Dealing with Anxiety

Recent Titles in Psychology Briefs

Understanding Depression
Rudy Nydegger

Suicide Prevention
Kristine Bertini

DEALING WITH ANXIETY

Rudy Nydegger

Psychology Briefs

An Imprint of ABC-CLIO, LLC

Santa Barbara, California • Denver, Colorado

Library of Congress Cataloging-in-Publication Data

Nydegger, Rudy V., 1943-
   Dealing with anxiety / Rudy Nydegger.
     pages cm. — (Psychology briefs)
   Includes bibliographical references and index.
   ISBN 978-1-4408-4234-4 (hardback) — ISBN 978-1-4408-4235-1 (ebook)
1. Anxiety disorders.   2. Anxiety disorders—Treatment.   I. Title.
   RC531.N92 2016
   616.85'22—dc23   2015036587

ISBN: 978-1-4408-4234-4
EISBN: 978-1-4408-4235-1

20 19 18 17 16   1 2 3 4 5

This book is also available on the World Wide Web as an eBook.
Visit www.abc-clio.com for details.

Praeger
An Imprint of ABC-CLIO, LLC

ABC-CLIO, LLC
130 Cremona Drive, P.O. Box 1911
Santa Barbara, California 93116-1911

This book is printed on acid-free paper ∞

Manufactured in the United States of America

Contents

Preface

Anxiety and stress have been a part of the human experience at least since the beginning of recorded history and are very common today. Through research and education we are more aware of how they affect many different parts of our lives—work, school, family, friends, and even recreational activities. Some people, however, may be unaware of the extent to which positive and negative stress affects their health and daily decisions. It is typical for people to deny, ignore, distort, or misunderstand symptoms of anxiety and stress, which is one of the reasons why anxiety and stress-related conditions are frequently untreated.

People who are dealing with worries and difficulties in their lives seldom find comfort from others trying to cheer them up by saying things like, "Well, you think your life is bad, look at Charlie—his life is falling apart!" Perhaps the comment was meant to be a source of comfort, but, personally, someone else's misery has never made me feel better about a situation in my life. If it was as easy as, "Just don't think about it!" or "Look on the bright side!" or even, "Don't worry, things will eventually get better!" very few of us would ever experience feelings of anxiety for very long.

Life is filled with normal anxieties and stressors, but many people live with a higher and prolonged level of anxiety identified as a type of a diagnosable illness called an "anxiety disorder." This book examines the world of anxiety—including the definition and explanation of its effects, the important differences between "normal" anxiety and true clinical disorders, and how it is diagnosed and treated. In some communities, people worry from day to day that they will not have enough to eat, a safe place to stay, and the necessities to sustain life. Others worry about their medical conditions, relationships, family problems, or world events. One of the differences between anxieties of today and those of the past is the growing number of things that worry us, as well as the complex way that many different things can affect our lives. Today's world is more dynamic with the rate of change increasing faster than in previous decades. For example, how many changes in daily living do you think occurred between April 3, 1201, and April 3, 1301, in most parts of the world? How much change has occurred in the lives of people in the developed countries from April 3, 1915, to April 3, 2015? The number of changes that occurred this year is higher than those of last year and even more will take place next year. The compounded rate of change is itself a major source of stress and anxiety for many people, and it promises to worsen in all parts of the world.

Learning how to recognize and deal with stress, worry, and anxiety is an important challenge for all of us, but for those who struggle with anxiety disorders, the difference between managing these disorders and not seeking treatment may be the difference between living a normal, productive, and reasonably happy life and being chronically miserable, uncomfortable, and unproductive. This book examines the issues of living with anxiety and anxiety-related disorders. Chapter 1 defines the term "anxiety" and explains how it feels and how it can affect us. Diagnostic issues and controversies related to the detection, diagnosis, and treatment of anxiety and related disorders are discussed, as well as myths and misunderstandings about these conditions. Although everyone has felt anxious or worried at some time, few people understand the real difference between normal worrying and a diagnosable anxiety disorder.

Chapter 2 discusses who is more likely to develop anxiety disorders and the costs associated with these types of problems, as well as the challenges faced when identifying, diagnosing, and treating different types of individuals. Anxiety disorders can appear to be similar across cultures or groups, but the differing rates at which anxiety occurs is often unique in some communities and the types of effective treatments can differ as well. Finally, anxiety disorders can appear to be different depending upon a person's gender, age, race, or culture.

Anxiety disorders can affect people personally, socially, at work, and in school, and can impact them in terms of lost work time due to treatment appointments or absenteeism, disability, decreased productivity, and conflicts at work or school as well as within families. Many must also deal with lost dreams of success and damaged or ruined careers and lives. Yet, there seems to be minimal public awareness or concern about the challenges of anxiety disorders and how they affect the daily lives of millions of people. Even more troubling is that today there are many different and effective treatments that can minimize and control the misery, expense, and other problems caused by anxiety disorders. Unfortunately, treatments are often inaccessible in some communities, many people may not know where to find appropriate treatment, they cannot access the treatment that might be available, or they may avoid it due to social or cultural stigmas.

Chapter 3 addresses the interesting and controversial issues surrounding the origin and causes of anxiety disorders. Psychological theories range from the psychodynamic, such as Freudian psychoanalysis, to the behavioral approaches and the newer cognitive and cognitive/behavioral approaches, as well as to the Humanistic and Existential theories. In addition, we will explore some of the sociological and cultural theories and how they impact our understanding of the development and treatment of anxiety disorders. How a society/culture views, manages, and pays for the treatment of psychological problems varies widely and is relevant to understanding the causes of anxiety disorders. However, these factors alone do not adequately explain the cause, manifestation, types, and treatments of anxiety-related conditions.

This chapter also examines some of the biological types of theories of anxiety disorders. Genetic factors as well as theories that rely on explanations based on chemicals in the brain and various hormones are also addressed. Finally, there is also a discussion regarding the things that make some people more vulnerable to developing an anxiety disorder.

The three chapters that follow will discuss in depth the different types of anxiety disorders and how these are diagnosed and differ from one another. There is also a thorough discussion of the specific issues faced by people suffering from each of these disorders and the kinds of treatments that might be used to help people who are suffering from them.

Chapter 7 examines the most recent research literature on the available and experimental treatments for anxiety disorders and explores the advantages and disadvantages of the different types of treatments and the issues involved with their use. Biological, psychological, and alternative treatments are all explored.

In Chapter 8 issues confronting patients and families of patients with anxiety disorders are addressed. Details about the things that patients and families can do to cope with, help treat, and even prevent some of the problems and complications that are part of having and living with an anxiety disorder are addressed and discussed.

The last chapter of the book will summarize the issues that were addressed in the book and will also discuss some of the treatment, clinical, social, and political issues involved in dealing with these different types of disorders. Finally, the appendix at the end of the book lists books, articles, organizations, and websites that will provide additional resources for people who want or need more information or support as they confront and deal with their anxiety and related disorders. There are also reference notes that refer to sources that were used in each chapter in the book.

1

❖

What Is Anxiety?

Anxiety is the one state no one wants to visit. It can take the best of times and make them a terrifying blur of the worst feelings imaginable. It makes you want—no, need—to find comfort from anything or anyone, and that is always the wrong thing to do. Anxiety is truly one of the demons of existence.

This description of anxiety describes an uncomfortable experience that most people have felt at one time or another. References to anxiety and fear are found historically in all cultures, and evidence suggests that they exist across species. The "fight or flight" reaction is an evolutionary adaptation that helps to protect an organism from harm and mobilizes the body for a quick response. When we feel frightened or anxious our body readies itself to take action—to resist/fight a threat or to escape/flee from it. However, many people experience intense feelings of anxiety that emerge even when no actual danger is present and yet the body and mind still react as if truly threatened.

Anxiety is a result of the *perception* of threat or danger and is open to wide misinterpretation or distortion. In most cases, anxiety is a future-oriented problem, worrying about something that "might" happen or exaggerating a perceived future threat. When the intensity and duration of the fear is greater than the real threat, anxiety is considered maladaptive and unhealthy. Feeling nervous about an upcoming event is certainly normal, but if the anxiety becomes so severe that it prevents us from following through with the event as planned, then the anxiety has developed into a significant problem.

My own definition of anxiety is, "a state of arousal that is subjectively experienced as aversive." In addition, anxiety usually includes feelings of apprehension, uncertainty, and/or fear, as well as negative thinking. When we are excited about something our physical reactions are similar to those experienced when we are anxious, but we interpret them very differently. Whether we identify our feelings as anxiety or excitement depends upon the events leading up to those feelings, as well as the subjective interpretation of that event or situation.

Symptoms of anxiety include irritability, intense fear, worry, difficulty concentrating, and a general "keyed up" feeling. Physical symptoms of anxiety often include sweating, dry mouth, hot flashes or chills, dizziness, heart palpitations, muscle tension, trembling, nausea, and restlessness. When anxiety is severe, lasts for a long time or frequently recurs, and is disruptive to a person's life and sense of comfort it may be a diagnosable anxiety disorder. Understandably, people who suffer from anxiety disorders want desperately to make these feelings and symptoms disappear. One of the best descriptions of severe anxiety is the overwhelming *fear of the loss of control*. This sensation is one of receiving a flood of powerful and crushing negative feelings, or of dying or "losing my mind," that seems completely out of one's control.

THE AGE OF ANXIETY

Many say that we live in an "Age of Anxiety," which may seem a bit peculiar considering the numerous comforts and conveniences available to many of us living in a developed country. Why then do people who live in relative comfort still experience anxiety to a degree that incapacitates them? The answer is that some people suffer from an anxiety disorder, which is the result of a disproportionate response to a *perceived threat* rather than a rational appraisal and response to a *real threat*. Living with an anxiety disorder is not the same thing as experiencing "normal" feelings of anxiety.

Research indicates that Americans have shifted toward higher levels of anxiety in recent decades with people in all age groups reporting clinically relevant anxiety more often than ever before. Although this may be due to an increased awareness about mental health issues and more frequently reporting problems, studies show that both children and college students experienced a substantial rate increase in anxiety between 1952 and 1993, with no indication that this trend has or will subside. During the 1980s the average American child reported more anxiety than child patients of the 1950s, leading some professionals to feel that a decrease in social connectedness during our modern times may be responsible for increases in reported anxiety while others believe that the world is more dangerous and that increased anxiety is understandable. Of course, over the past few decades economic uncertainty, safety concerns, social acceptance, and job security were and are sources of stress, but none of these is a major factor in the rise of diagnosed anxiety disorders. The increasing rate of reported anxiety disorders in recent years appears to have affected men and women equally, although women still suffer anxiety disorders more often than men, and at about the same rate as in the past. Many authors agree that the 20th century should be referred to as the "Age of Anxiety"; it remains to be determined if the 21st century will follow suit.

One major difficulty in dealing with anxiety is the manner in which people attempt to control it. I often tell patients who suffer from an anxiety disorder that, "Anything you are presently doing to make yourself feel better is probably the wrong thing to do." That may sound strange, but when we typically rush to take action without thinking, we often worsen a situation. Likewise, when people notice that feelings of anxiety are beginning to overwhelm them, they want to stop them as quickly as possible. Unfortunately, whatever they typically do will only briefly and temporarily alleviate the anxiety. Some may resort to drugs and/or alcohol in order to "self-medicate" the anxiety away, but this only works temporarily and often makes the anxiety worse. Others may focus their attention on TV, the computer, video games, texting, talking on the phone, and shopping to distract them from the anxiety, and others may find refuge in food, smoking, or sex. In an effort to "control" the anxiety, some may display an artificial air of calmness and simply deny that a problem exists. This may at first appear to be someone who is "coping," but in reality it is often only denial. An additional misleading "coping strategy" that can develop into a serious issue is the intentional changing of one's plans or daily routine in order to avoid situations that might produce feelings of anxiety. However, the true source of the anxiety is not the planned event but rather the person's underlying and unrealistic fears in anticipation of the situation. Once you have felt better by having avoided one event, you will then go on to miss a second and third event where feelings of anxiety will surface; now you have more than two situations that you will need to elude in order to avoid feeling uncomfortable. The pattern continues until you only have a few places where you can go and feel comfortable—sometimes only at home—and this now becomes a new problem.

DIAGNOSING ANXIETY DISORDERS

In addition to being upsetting and intrusive to one's life, anxiety disorders are challenging to diagnose. First, it is necessary to determine if the varying levels of anxiety and fear that people experience are a "normal" reaction or if they reach the threshold of a diagnosable condition. Research clearly demonstrates that anxiety can be reliably and validly assessed, but that does not mean that it is a simple process; the diagnosis primarily relies upon the clinical judgment of well-trained professionals.

The next challenge when evaluating the symptoms of an anxiety disorder is to rule out alternative diagnoses. Since many symptoms of anxiety are physical in nature, the diagnosing professional must consider and ultimately rule out any physical diagnoses as well as alternative psychological diagnoses, and often the collaboration of professionals from different disciplines is helpful or necessary in order to make a valid diagnosis. When people are acutely anxious, their heart may pound and they may feel as though they are having trouble breathing, both possible signs of a serious medical issue. A medical doctor may suspect that a patient's symptoms are due to anxiety, but they will often run some tests in order to rule out medical problems. For example, someone who is very anxious may report a headache, hot and cold flashes, and nausea—is it anxiety or a virus or some other infection? In addition to physical signs and symptoms, anxiety may accompany other psychological problems, and the diagnostician must be certain that the presenting symptoms of anxiety cannot be better explained by a different diagnosis.

Finally, the professional must evaluate the severity and unique features of the symptoms to determine if there is a possibility of an illness in addition to the anxiety problem. Other medical or psychological illnesses that are present at the same time as the primary diagnosed condition are known as "comorbid" conditions. Comorbid conditions can often complicate the process of assessing, diagnosing, and treating patients with anxiety disorder. However, it is critical that professionals establish a clear diagnostic picture in order to correctly treat any and all of the presenting and relevant conditions.

While anxiety is a most uncomfortable and sometimes frightening condition, it often goes without benefit of a diagnosis or adequate treatment. Those who choose to seek help usually begin with a visit to their primary care physician (PCP), who will first try to rule out physical causes for the symptoms. The PCP may tell the patient that it is nothing serious and to wait to see if the symptoms go away on their own. The PCP might also prescribe a psychotropic medication (for psychiatric symptoms) that should ease the burden of the symptoms, a reasonable strategy—particularly on a short-term basis. However, medication alone is never adequate treatment for an anxiety disorder. Finally, the PCP can refer the patient to a psychologist, psychiatrist, or other appropriate mental health professional for further medication consultation, psychotherapy, or both.

MYTHS ABOUT ANXIETY

Understanding the nature and impact of anxiety disorders means separating the many myths and misconceptions from the facts. Popular thinking and discussions on these issues is rarely based on modern theories and research and is not usually consistent with standard diagnostic criteria. Therefore, we will address some of the myths and the facts that will hopefully clarify them.

Myth: Anxiety Conditions Are Rare

Fact: Although the majority of people do not suffer from a diagnosable anxiety disorder, these types of disorders are not rare. About 19 million Americans suffer from a clinically relevant anxiety disorder, and it is likely that you know someone who lives with severe anxiety. A list of well-known people who have publicly acknowledged dealing with anxiety disorder is presented at the end of this chapter.

Myth: Anxiety Disorders Are Not Illnesses

Fact: Although anxiety disorders are not caused by a particular germ or passed around like a cold virus, they are legitimate psychiatric illnesses identified by a specific set of symptoms and diagnostic criteria. It is also true that psychological as well as physical factors are involved in the development of anxiety disorders.

Myth: Only One Type of Anxiety Disorder Exists

Fact: There are several categories and types of anxiety disorders, each differing in appearance and symptoms, course and progression, and in the types of treatments required. Although debilitating anxiety is common to all anxiety disorders, these problems often appear quite differently in different people, who each cope with their anxiety disorder in various ways.

Myth: An Anxiety Disorder Is a Fixed Element of Personality

Fact: Although some people are more inclined to feel anxious as part of their personality, an anxiety disorder is not a component of one's personality but rather is acquired *in addition to* the personality. Anyone can develop an anxiety disorder, and some may be more prone than others due to genetics, past experiences, or even their personality. But an anxiety disorder is not an ingrained, fundamental part of an individual's personality. Treating an anxiety disorder means reducing and controlling the symptoms, not changing the personality itself. Certainly in the process of treatment a person may make some significant and important changes, but treatment does not involve a "personality transplant."

Myth: Emotionally Immature People Develop Anxiety Disorders

Fact: There is absolutely no relationship between emotional maturity and the development of an anxiety disorder. The causes of these types of disorders are based entirely upon other factors and do not reflect someone's level of maturity, their accomplishments, or their personal strengths or convictions. Strength lies in seeking treatment, not in denying the need for it. Women are more frequently diagnosed with anxiety disorders at least in part because they are more willing to receive treatment and are also more often affected by complex factors such as genetics and social roles. These will be discussed in depth later in this book.

Myth: Parents Cause Anxiety Disorders

Fact: Developing an anxiety disorder involves complex processes and does not arise from a single or simple source. Rarely do all of the children within one family develop anxiety disorders, regardless of the shared environment. Children of conscientious parents can develop anxiety disorders, while children of less competent parents can grow up without an anxiety disorder and vice versa. While all parents can look back and think of things they might have done differently, their treatment of their children cannot be the *only* factor that produces anxiety disorders. However, genetic factors can certainly be a factor to consider when noting frequent occurrences of anxiety disorder within one family.

Myth: Medical Conditions Cause Anxiety Attacks

Fact: Although anxiety attacks exhibit physical symptoms, including racing or irregular heartbeat, trouble breathing, and chest pain, they are not the result of a physical problem such as a heart attack. Still, many frightened people who are gasping for breath and consumed by thoughts of imminent death rush to a hospital emergency room believing that they are having a heart attack or some other catastrophic medical emergency. At such times, it is difficult to remember that *no one has ever died as a result of an anxiety attack*. People who have never experienced an anxiety attack cannot even imagine the terrifying and intense feelings and symptoms that are involved.

Myth: Avoiding Stressful Situations Controls Anxiety Attacks

Fact: Avoiding more and more situations perceived to be responsible for feelings of severe anxiety will not alleviate symptoms but rather make them worse. Treatment methods are intended to support a person while confronting difficult or new situations rather than avoiding them. Focusing on efforts to *not* avoid those situations that produce severe anxiety is a major component of psychological treatments for anxiety disorders.

Myth: Intense Feelings of Anxiety Means the Person Is Losing Control

Fact: The most significant word in understanding severe anxiety is the *fear* of losing control, not actually losing control. A person may feel like they cannot control what is happening to them, but in reality they *do* have control over their own behavior as well as control over their reactions to the fear and/or anxiety they are experiencing. In fact, most treatments for anxiety disorders are based upon methods that teach a person how to gain control over their actions, thoughts, and feelings within their own unique circumstances in order to reduce and/or eliminate the anxiety.

Myth: You Can Pass Out during an Anxiety Attack

Fact: An anxiety attack does not by itself cause someone to faint. However, if someone is hyperventilating (breathing too fast for too long), they may become light-headed and could possibly briefly lose consciousness, although this is truly very rare. Even if this were to occur, for example when driving a car, you would have plenty of time to pull the car over to a stop. Refusing to drive a car and isolating at home is a good example of how the *fear* of having an anxiety attack could lead to additional problems. That is why treatment involves helping people learn how to avoid or minimize the intensity of an anxiety attack using psychological techniques.

Myth: Responsible People Often Worry

Fact: Acting responsibly has nothing to do with worrying. However, frequent worrying has a lot to do with being continuously anxious. People who are chronic worriers often spend inordinate amounts of time thinking about things they cannot do anything about. Focusing one's time and actions on those issues that are under your own control is a much more constructive use of one's energy. One step in the treatment for anxiety disorders is learning how to avoid unnecessary worrying.

Myth: Worrying May Prevent an Unwanted Event from Occurring

Fact: This is called *superstitious thinking* and is clearly not rational. Most people realize that what they are thinking has nothing to do with when or why things happen. However, some people justify chronic worrying by explaining that it prepares them to deal with a feared, unwanted outcome more effectively than being surprised by it. But being prepared is not equivalent to worrying about an event until it finally occurs. Continuous thinking and worrying about the worse-case scenario is not realistic or healthy and is a waste of time and energy. It does not produce the necessary skills or motivation to confront and deal with problems and can lead to needless, dysfunctional symptoms and to avoidance.

Myth: Thinking Positive Thoughts Eliminates Anxiety Disorders

Fact: Depending upon positive thinking as a cure for an anxiety disorder is similar to superstitious thinking (as mentioned above). Trying to control anxiety by thinking "happy thoughts" may temporarily alleviate some feelings of stress, but it is not a cure. Thinking about something does not change the occurrence or outcome of an event—it is not what we think but rather what we do about those thoughts that actually makes changes in our lives. However, some benefits of positive thinking are proving to be important in terms of treatment, theory, and research. Learning to control our actions, thoughts, and feelings is a productive and significant element of most treatment methods, but positive thinking is not a treatment by itself.

Myth: Identifying the Original Cause "Fixes" an Anxiety Disorder

Fact: Over time an anxiety disorder becomes "functionally autonomous," which means that it exists independently of its original cause(s). Behavior patterns that develop help us to "practice" the anxiety symptoms over a lifetime and need to be addressed, regardless of the precipitating events or remote history behind them. Fragmented and inaccurate memories cannot produce a reliable picture of past personal events, and focusing only upon the suspected "source" of the anxiety disorder is rarely effective or helpful treatment. In addition, the original cause of an anxiety disorder may never be discovered. However, it does serve the entertainment industry well, as is often seen in movies or TV shows where the "super shrink" identifies the hidden cause of a person's lifetime of misery and through the magical and powerful "treatment du jour" (treatment of the day) the character is miraculously "cured" and lives happily ever after. If it was only that simple!

Myth: Medications Mask Symptoms and Don't Cure Anxiety Disorders

Fact: Some people believe that you cannot treat anxiety disorders with medication because the drug only covers up the symptom and prevents actual treatment from working. In reality, prescription drugs are not a cure but rather a tool, preferably used in conjunction with psychotherapy to reduce, control, and eliminate symptoms of severe anxiety. Using medication as the *only* treatment over a long period may result in the return of anxiety disorder symptoms once the medication is discontinued. Occasionally, medication alone may be adequate treatment for someone who develops an anxiety disorder in reaction to a specific and recent situation but only on a short-term basis. Recent evidence suggests that when used improperly, medications can interfere with the effectiveness and long-term benefits of psychotherapy, which is why the psychologist/therapist and prescribing professional must work together.

Myth: Simple and Easy Treatments for Anxiety Are Available

Fact: Anxiety disorders are complex and their treatments are not simple or easy. When you read or hear, "Get rid of your anxiety in a matter of hours or days: just buy this book, and your problems will be over"—save your money! Quick cures found on the Internet, as well as promises for a "new" treatment, which psychologists and psychiatrists are somehow unaware of, often dupe unsuspecting people into wasting money and hope on worthless and potentially damaging information. Also, cults and cult-like organizations, claiming to have developed successful treatments for psychological problems such as anxiety, induce desperate people to pay large sums of money in exchange for a "cure." It cannot be stressed enough that both the development of and treatment for anxiety disorders involve complex processes that cannot be understood or treated with simple-minded and unrealistic methods that were designed primarily to separate people from their money.

Myth: Only Treatment "X" Is Effective on Anxiety Disorders

Fact: There are no two patients alike, and the treatment that works for one may not work for another. Experienced professionals know which types of therapies and medications are most likely to work and will develop a treatment plan that carefully considers the full range of possibilities. They must discuss the treatment plan with the patient, including both the benefits and potential risks of treatment options, make a recommendation, and then begin treatment.

Summary

Learning the facts about anxiety disorders will help you to begin to understand what causes them, how they are treated, and how they affect us. Having accurate information can help someone seek needed treatment; read, talk to your friends who are in treatment, and discuss issues or ask questions of your primary care physician and other professionals.

PEOPLE WHO SUFFER FROM ANXIETY DISORDERS

Everyone knows at least one person who suffers from an anxiety disorder, although you might not know it by looking at them. With treatment, most people can live normal lives whether the anxiety is an acute or chronic problem. Learning how to control and minimize the symptoms is one of the fundamental elements of treatment; being able to effectively deal with situations that produce anxiety is the other.

In addition to negotiating lives without the normal boundaries of privacy, a number of famous and talented people suffer from anxiety disorders. Some of these celebrities have been forthcoming about their condition, and their openness has given hope to others who deal with similar disorders. Many historical figures have been written about or have themselves written about their own personal challenges with anxiety disorders. The following list of well-known people who suffer from anxiety disorders gives you an idea of how widespread and common these problems are:

- Alanis Morissette (singer)
- Anthony Hopkins (actor)

- Aretha Franklin (singer)
- Barbara Bush (former first lady of the United States)
- Barbra Streisand (singer, actor)
- Bonnie Raitt (musician)
- Burt Reynolds (actor)
- Carly Simon (singer)
- Charlotte Brontë (author)
- Cher (singer, actor)
- Courtney Love (singer, actor)
- David Bowie (singer, actor)
- Donnie Osmond (singer, actor)
- Earl Campbell (football player, Heisman Trophy winner)
- Emily Dickinson (poet, writer)
- Eric Clapton (musician)
- Goldie Hawn (actor)
- Howard Stern (radio celebrity)
- Howie Mandel (comedian, TV host)
- Isaac Asimov (author)
- James Garner (actor)
- Joan Rivers (comedian)
- John Madden (former NFL coach, sports announcer)
- John Steinbeck (author)
- Johnny Depp (actor)
- Kim Basinger (actor)
- Marie Osmond (singer, entertainer)
- Michael Crichton (author)
- Michael Jackson (singer, entertainer)
- Naomi Judd (singer)
- Nicholas Cage (actor)
- Nicole Kidman (actor)
- Oprah Winfrey (TV host)
- Ray Charles (musician)
- Ricky Williams (NFL football player)
- Sally Field (actor)
- Sheryl Crow (musician)
- Sigmund Freud (psychoanalyst)

A specific type of anxiety disorder called obsessive-compulsive disorder (OCD) will be explained later in this book. Some celebrities who suffer from OCD include:

- Albert Einstein (physicist)
- Alec Baldwin (actor)
- Billy Bob Thornton (actor)
- Cameron Diaz (actor)
- Charles Darwin (scientist, author)
- Charlie Sheen (actor)
- Dan Ackroyd (actor)
- David Beckham (professional soccer player)
- Donald Trump (businessman, entrepreneur, political candidate)
- Fred Durst (musician)
- Harrison Ford (actor)
- Jennifer Love Hewitt (actor)
- Justin Timberlake (singer, entertainer)
- Kathie Lee Gifford (TV host)
- Leonardo DiCaprio (actor)
- Ludwig van Beethoven (composer)
- Martin Scorsese (director, producer)
- Michelangelo (artist, engineer)
- Penelope Cruz (actor)
- Roseanne Barr (comedian)
- Woody Allen (actor, director)

It is encouraging to see how many accomplished people have success-fully dealt with anxiety in their lives. Some types of anxiety disorders are more chronic than others, but it is possible to receive treatment that will help to manage and even "cure" the problem. A chronic psychological condition requires similar and continuous monitoring as does a chronic medical condition such as diabetes—if you take care of yourself and are compliant with treatment, you can live a normal and fulfilling life.

2

Anxiety Disorders: Who Gets Them and What Does It Cost?

Feeling anxious or nervous at times is quite common, but that does not mean that we all live with anxiety disorders. However, these disorders are not rare and affect almost 30 million Americans at some point in their lives. Estimations for the cost of anxiety disorders are about $46.6 billion annually, which is 31.5 percent of all expenses for mental illness in the United States. Less than 25 percent of these expenses are associated with medical or psychological treatments; more than 75 percent reflect the patients' and families' lost income and reduced productivity at work or school.

Although many suffer from anxiety disorders, it is troubling that so few of them receive appropriate treatment. It is estimated that of all those who suffer from a diagnosable anxiety disorder less than 25 percent will receive adequate treatment. Over the course of a whole lifetime slightly over 20 percent of men and 30 percent of women will develop a diagnosable anxiety disorder, which means that the cost of treatment and other expenses can become a significant financial burden.

GENDER AND ANXIETY DISORDERS

Women and Anxiety

Women of all ages suffer from anxiety disorders more frequently than men, with symptoms varying slightly between them. The reasons can be complicated, and some research suggests that fluctuations in the level of female reproductive hormones may have an effect on anxiety. Frequently, women experiencing hormonal changes (e.g., premenstrual, menopausal) may be more prone to anxiety, but varying hormone levels are not the only cause for increased anxiety. Social, cultural, and personal reasons, as well as some genetic components, contribute to an increase in the occurrence of anxiety in women. While most research on anxiety has been conducted in the United States and Western Europe, one's gender is significant in studying health issues around the world and in one's ability to receive adequate care. For example, in some countries women are not allowed to visit medical doctors or mental health professionals.

Men and Anxiety

Although there is no simple explanation as to why, men are less likely to be diagnosed with an anxiety disorder. However, significant numbers of men do experience anxiety but often choose not to seek help due to the "stigma" of having a condition that implies weakness or frailty. Professionals sometimes do not recognize symptoms of anxiety in male patients because the complaints men report are more likely to be physical symptoms than feelings of fear or anxiety. Typically, men who are brought to an emergency room with symptoms of a panic attack are more likely to be suspected of having a heart attack than being acutely anxious, although the opposite is true for women. Men are also more likely to "self-medicate" with alcohol and/or drugs, which could mask or distort symptoms of anxiety and lead to misdiagnoses.

There is not one definitive explanation that accounts for the variety of experiences and symptoms found in men and women suffering from anxiety disorders. Some biological differences may predispose women to having anxiety-related problems, but this alone is not an adequate explanation. If we consider all of the risk factors for developing anxiety disorders—biological, psychological, social, cultural, and others—we can conclude that, the *more* and/or *more severe* risk factors to which a person is exposed, the greater the chance that a person will develop a disorder. Women generally tend to have more risk factors and are, therefore, more likely to develop anxiety disorders. It is encouraging to note that even if men are less likely to seek treatment, they are just as likely to respond positively to treatment and will show as significant an improvement in their condition as women.

CHILDREN AND TEENS AND ANXIETY

Specific fears and social fears are common among young children, but most will outgrow them as they mature. Other than separation anxiety disorder, which is specific to children, youngsters experience the same types of anxiety disorders as do adults. One of the differences between children and adults, when considering fears and phobias, is that children are less likely to recognize that their fears are excessive or unrealistic. For many children their fears are associated with school and school-related activities, and it is not uncommon for children to report being fearful of changing clothes for gym class, eating in the cafeteria, speaking in front of the class, and other typical school activities. It is also not unusual for children to feign illness in order to stay at home and avoid the situations that frighten them. Some studies have shown no difference between boys and girls with respect to the types of anxiety disorders they experience, while others have demonstrated differences. The most important finding is that if they receive appropriate treatment they are both likely to improve.

Diagnosing anxiety disorders in children is challenging because many of their symptoms are somatic (physical) in nature. The most common symptoms reported by children with anxiety disorders are restlessness, stomachaches, blushing, palpitations, muscle tension, sweating, and trembling/shaking. Boys and girls present approximately the same number of symptoms, although boys tend to report stomachaches and chest pains more frequently than girls and older children typically report more symptoms than the younger ones. It is also true that children in highly stressful environments are more likely to develop anxiety disorders than those in calmer and less difficult circumstances.

In teens the rate of anxiety disorders is relatively high, and their anxiety symptoms show higher rates of stress and family dysfunction, which is similar to children. Interestingly, teens with anxiety disorders report less peer contact than other teens, which may be due to their anxiety causing them to avoid contact with others. Although anxious teens may intentionally avoid peer contact and conflict, peer conflict is probably not the major cause of the anxiety they are experiencing; the avoidance of peers is more likely a symptom of anxiety than the cause of the anxiety disorder.

In college students the patterns in anxiety disorders are similar to those in older teens and younger adults. As might be anticipated, anxiety problems can negatively affect interpersonal relations, emotions, and personal rela-tionships. The more anxiety they experience, the more difficulties they will have in school and with social activities. One advantage for college students is the availability of an on-campus student health center or a university (college) counseling center where they can seek help and advice. One additional risk for college students is the easy access to alcohol or drugs as a way of coping with their anxiety instead of seeking treatment.

One of the difficulties in diagnosing and treating anxiety disorders is the frequency of patients having comorbidities (other conditions requir-ing treatment), and in youths with anxiety disorders comorbidities are the rule, not the exception. A typical complication of anxiety disorders in children and youths is the presence of sleep-related problems (SRPs). Although sometimes considered a comorbid condition, SRPs are more often a direct result of the anxiety disorder and are almost always present. SRPs are also significant predictors of anxiety severity and of family func-tioning in the home. Typically, when youngsters are treated for anxiety conditions they do improve, and the SRPs associated with the anxiety disorder get better as well.

Diagnosing and Treating Children and Teens

It is not uncommon for anxiety disorders in children to go unrecognized or to be written off as part of some other problem. However, it is impor-tant to remember that childhood anxiety disorders are not just "normal development" and need to be diagnosed and treated early and effectively. If they are not treated properly, the quality of the child's life and their psychological development will be affected. Untreated anxiety disorders in children make it more likely that they will develop anxiety disorders as adults.

Treatments that are endorsed by mental health professionals and that are available to children and teens with anxiety disorders include medica-tions together with cognitive-behavioral therapy (CBT). However, youths and their parents are often initially less accepting of these types of treatments and are more likely to embrace informal support from family, friends, and support groups as a "treatment" for anxiety disorders. Parents are frequently reluctant to approve medication and CBT because they feel that their acceptance of such treatments is a formal admission that their child does not simply have a minor problem that they will eventually "outgrow," but rather an important condition that needs addressing; they also often have concerns about the risks of taking medications. Profes-sionals must educate patients, friends, and families about the benefits of early recognition and treatment and encourage questions and discussions regarding treatment options. Support offered by family and friends to patients dealing with anxiety problems can be helpful, but this is not a substitute for professional treatment.

ANXIETY DISORDERS IN THE ELDERLY

Although depression is considered a common problem among the elderly, anxiety is more frequently challenging to them and affects between 10–24 percent of older individuals. One difficulty in detecting and diagnosing anxiety problems in the elderly is that they often report physical symptoms of anxiety rather than the psychological and emotional ones, similarly to children.

In older patients anxiety is associated with diminished well-being and increased disability, and, while the use of general health services increases among elderly anxiety sufferers, the commitment to appropriate mental health care is typically low. This could be the result of a lack of understanding about anxiety disorder but is more likely due to a minimal number of valid diagnoses and treatment referrals. Providers sometimes consider symptoms of anxiety in the elderly an understandable reaction to life's frequently negative events in this age group, but the symptoms experienced are virtually the same as others who suffer from anxiety disorders who have experienced few negative life events. Regardless of the source of the anxiety, the elderly are deserving of and can benefit from effective treatment as well as any other type of patient.

Although anxiety is a common and debilitating problem in the elderly, it is frequently overlooked or dismissed by providers, family, and friends. In addition, the majority of the elderly with anxiety disorders suffer from at least one comorbid psychological problem, which increases their risk of physical disability, memory problems, a reduced quality of life, and even death. Diagnosing anxiety disorders in the elderly is also more challenging because the symptoms are usually physical in nature and are often vague and difficult to differentiate from other physical or psychological problems. Further, anxiety can exacerbate the symptoms of other medical disorders, making them more difficult to treat.

Anxiety disorders in older people can and should be treated, although treatment response and follow-through is often lower than in other age groups due to several factors. First, people from older generations are generally less aware of psychological issues and are more likely to blame their anxiety symptoms on an illness or physical condition or on others. Second, transportation issues and financial concerns may present problems in seeking treatment. Third, taking medication for an anxiety disorder, which is often used as the first line of treatment, is often not as effective in older people. With lower metabolic rates, they are more likely to experience negative side effects and less likely to tolerate a therapeutic dosage level. Some of the side effects, such as drowsiness and impaired balance and cognitive function, can be dangerous. Due to other medical conditions, older people often take a variety of medications, and these may interact with the psychotropic (psychiatric) drugs, producing unwanted side effects. However, the elderly tend to respond well to psychotherapy along with a low dose of medication as treatment for anxiety. CBT is now considered by most practitioners as the first line of treatment for anxiety disorders in the elderly. While the combination of CBT and medication works well, for both the general population and specifically for elderly patients with anxiety disorders, many studies suggest that most of the improvement in these patients is primarily due to the psychotherapy.

Clearly, anxiety disorders are common and problematic among the elderly, but research on the course and treatment lags well behind other conditions in older adults. Anxiety disorders are as common in older adults as in other age groups, and they typically suffer from both anxiety and depression; females who have less education have an increased risk for developing both problems.

RACE, ETHNICITY, AND ANXIETY DISORDERS

There is evidence of anxiety and fear-based psychological problems within all cultures. They may be identified by different names or be perceived differently, and the availability of care may be quite different, but no culture is immune. This makes understanding and comparing anxiety among cultures challenging and complex, since behavior in one culture might be indicative of anxiety but in another it may mean something quite different.

African Americans and Anxiety

African Americans experience anxiety disorders in different patterns, and their access to treatment is not generally equal to that of the majority of the Caucasian population. As with other groups, the stigma of mental illness prevents some African Americans from seeking care, even those with adequate health insurance. The disturbing fact that over 25 percent of African Americans do not have health insurance is significant as well. Only one third of African Americans who need care for anxiety disorders receive it, and they are more likely to terminate treatment prematurely.

Further, African Americans are more likely to receive temporary or inadequate mental health treatment at the primary care level, although proper treatments are as effective and successful for African Americans as white patients. Some professionals believe that significant racial differences in help-seeking behaviors and symptom presentation may be responsible for under-recognition and misdiagnosis of anxiety disorders among African American patients in outpatient mental health settings. In the primary care setting, African Americans more often report physical symptoms of anxiety disorders. Even when demographic and socioeconomic status (SES) are held constant, the racial differences for problems such as phobias still remain, strongly indicating that being an African American is one of the risk factors for phobias; other risk factors for phobia include being female, young, and having a lower education level.

Although the rate of panic disorder among African Americans and whites is similar, African Americans report more intense fears of dying or feelings of "going crazy," higher levels of numbing and tingling in their extremities, and higher rates of comorbid posttraumatic stress disorder (PTSD) and depression than white patients.

When examining the rates of anxiety disorders within different racial groups, it is important to recognize that all patients exhibit multiple and different risk factors, as well as various other medical and psychological disorders. Many people over the age of 65 who are evaluated for anxiety or depression are likely to show patterns of alcohol misuse, and about 59 percent are minorities. In contrast to the usually minimal treatment available at the primary care level, an integrated care setting that offers professional services in different specialties, such as alcohol and drug abuse counseling, typically provides much more responsive and coordinated care to patients and families. This is particularly important for minorities such as African Americans who are less frequently referred to specialists for mental health care.

Adequately diagnosing and treating anxiety disorders in all minority groups must be a priority—and certainly among African Americans for whom treatment rarely reaches the threshold for attaining good clinical results. A better understanding of the differences in symptom presentation and treatment options is critical in order to deal more effectively with these highly treatable conditions, and it is clear that with appropriate and adequate care, African Americans demonstrate the same rates of improvement and "cures" as do white people suffering from similar disorders. The key, then, is to provide patients with a proper diagnosis, a referral to the correct provider or specialist, appropriate treatment, and follow up and support for the patient over time.

Asian Americans and Anxiety

The research literature on anxiety has rarely focused on Asian Americans, but as an expanding cultural group that is presently underserved we need to learn more about their mental health needs, particularly those of older Asian Americans. Asian Americans scored higher on measures of depression and social anxiety and reported higher levels of distress than white Americans, with recent immigrants showing the highest levels of distress and demonstrating that Asian American ethnicity is related to social anxiety. They are under-represented among mental health professionals, which may make some Asian American patients reluctant to seek help.

Growing evidence supports the theory that ethnic differences affect the rates of social anxiety, and studies of college students consistently report that Asian American students experience higher levels of social anxiety than do European-American students. Interestingly, some cross-cultural data suggests that shyness and even social anxiety can be consistent with a culture's socialization patterns and is considered normal within some Asian groups. However, other research suggests that the experience of social anxiety is associated with subjective distress and functional impairment in Asian Americans. These subjects are rarely discussed with friends, however, because Asian students are more concerned with "losing face" and with trying to avoid negative evaluations by others than their white colleagues.

It appears that Asian American students are at significant risk for anxiety disorders and depression due to immigrant/minority status and cultural stressors. Other stressors such as academic problems and family pressure complicate the college experience for Asian Americans and can lead to increased difficulties. To fully appreciate the challenges Asian students face, unique cultural issues including a high emphasis on family loyalty and the adherence to collectivist values must be considered.

Attention has recently focused upon a specific cultural group, Japanese Americans, with some interesting findings. Japanese Americans conceptualize anxiety by describing more depressive symptoms than anxiety symptoms, especially among older Japanese American patients, making it difficult to accurately diagnose anxiety disorders. Also, Japanese Americans tend to report more cognitive symptoms than the somatic symptoms we find with other minority groups and in elder Americans. We know that specific phobias and related conditions exist within each culture, including Japan, but sometimes these conditions appear differently or have a different name.

Research in mental health regarding Asians rarely focuses on one specific Asian group, like the Japanese or Koreans, and instead, over forty distinctly different Asian ethnic groups are viewed as one homogeneous group. Most studies have focused on East Asians—including the Japanese, Chinese, and Koreans—and have neglected the Southeast Asians such as the Indians, Pakistanis, Bangladeshis, Nepalese, and Sri Lankans. Asian American women are particularly underrepresented in the literature, even though research consistently demonstrates that women worldwide are more at risk for anxiety and depression than are men.

When we group the Asian Americans with the American Pacific Islanders, we discover the lowest possible level of utilization of mental health services for any ethnic population, most likely due to cultural stigma and financial limitations. The poverty rate for this group is lower than the national poverty average. Asian American students experience discrimination like many ethnic minorities and are higher risk for anxiety as well as depression, suicidal ideation, and psychological distress. As might be expected, the perception of discrimination by a person of an ethnic minority is one factor contributing to their experienced stress and anxiety; these perceptions are directly related to frequent negative mental health outcomes.

Asians, and others who are foreign born, are becoming more prominent minorities in the United States and are receiving more attention in the research literature and in clinical settings. Since people from all cultures suffer from anxiety disorders, it is important to appreciate the ethnicity and cultural background of each patient prior to diagnosing and prescribing treatment. Cultural awareness and sensitivity are critical factors to providing reasonable, responsible, and appropriate mental health services.

Hispanic Americans and Anxiety

Like other minorities within the United States, Hispanics deal with ethnic-specific challenges with regard to social, medical, and mental health issues, including anxiety. Hispanics, like Asians, are not a homogeneous group and involve people from many different countries and cultures. However, they tend to be grouped together statistically in most research and demographic analyses. As a group, Hispanic Americans have the lowest per capita income of any minority group and are less likely to have health insurance—in fact, they are twice as likely to be uninsured as whites. Although the 1990 census reported that 40 percent of Hispanics could not speak English, only a few mental health providers can speak

Spanish. Interestingly, Hispanic immigrants have a lower rate of mental illness than those Hispanics born in the United States, and this finding suggests that difficulties with acculturation, discrimination, and immigrant status are related to their mental health difficulties. One study found that, when Asian American and Hispanic students are brought to the attention of school authorities, the Hispanic students are far more likely to be accused of wrongdoing such as cheating or breaking the law than the Asian students, and they are more likely to experience these events as stressful.

An interesting phenomenon called the "Latino Paradox" refers to the consistent finding that the mental health status of lower socioeconomic status (SES) Latinos tends to be better than that of low-SES whites or low-SES African Americans, and the risk for mental health problems within minority groups increases with the number of years lived in the United States. But, as mentioned above, treating Hispanics as a homogeneous group is misleading since significant differences exist by area of origin and degree of acculturation. For example, Puerto Rican mothers and fathers are more likely to meet the criteria for major depression and generalized anxiety disorder (GAD) than Hispanics from any other area. In fact, Puerto Rican Americans are at greatest risk for depression and anxiety disorders one year after the birth of a child, while Mexican Americans are at the lowest risk. The average risk of the two Hispanic groups taken together appears to be normal, but the differences between the cultural groups suggest that professionals may miss diagnosing anxiety disorder or depression due to being unfamiliar with each group's risk factors and symptoms.

Native Americans and Alaskan Natives and Anxiety

As with other minority groups, there is minimal comprehensive and appropriate research on the mental health needs and issues for Native Americans and Alaskan Natives. Past attempts to eradicate the culture of Native Americans have been associated with negative mental health consequences, and even when intentions were good, the results were quite harmful. During the late 19th and early to mid-20th centuries in many Midwestern and Southwestern states, "Indian Schools" were created and intended to bring education, literacy, and economic self-reliance to the Native people. However, the "education" element also included the conversion to Christianity and an effort to stamp out Native religious beliefs. State governments also tried to "help" the Native American children become like the white majority population, an effort believed by most whites to be positive. Largely, they succeeded in stripping the

Natives of their spiritual beliefs, language, culture, sense of heritage, and the support they should have received from their tribal groups.

Native Americans and Alaskan Natives are significantly impoverished with more than 25 percent living below the poverty level, and some studies found that negative mental health outcomes are related to their minority status and their financial and social hardships. Understandably, many people from minority groups would prefer to see a mental health provider from their own background but, unfortunately, there are few licensed mental health providers from Native American or Alaskan Native background. It is not surprising, then, that many people within minority groups like these seek advice from traditional healers within their own culture and, when available, will combine it with conventional care.

Summary on Ethnicity and Anxiety

In some Native American languages words for depression and anxiety do not even exist, but the suicide rate for Native American and Alaskan Native males between the ages of 15–24 is two to three times higher than the national rate. Mental health needs are not being recognized or addressed and adequate treatment is not being provided. Among Asian Americans and Pacific Islanders, the rate of mental illness is not that different from other Americans, but they have the lowest utilization rates of mental health services of any minority. Mexican-born Americans have a 25 percent rate of mental illness, while Mexicans born in the United States have a 48 percent rate—clearly, a growing and serious problem. Minorities are also overrepresented among the most vulnerable, high-need groups—such as the homeless and incarcerated persons—and these populations have a much higher rate of mental illness than people living "normally" in the community. These are clearly problems that deserve more attention.

HOMOSEXUAL GROUPS AND ANXIETY

Gay men and lesbian women are specific subgroups that have largely been ignored in the research, partially because they may not be recognized unless they identify themselves to treatment professionals. Data suggests, however, that levels of depression and anxiety in homosexual persons (whether HIV positive or negative) are substantially higher than in the heterosexual population. We also know from research that mood and anxiety disorders are more prevalent among those who have had one or more same-sex partners, including gay, lesbian, and bisexual individuals.

One encouraging fact is that the lesbian/gay/bisexual community is more likely to access mental health services than the heterosexual population and, therefore, is much more likely to benefit from treatment.

RELIGIOUS GROUPS AND ANXIETY

Religious groups have also received recent attention in the research literature. Religious beliefs themselves are not likely to be a risk factor, and even among people within the same religious group, beliefs can be fairly diverse. It appears that it is not the specific religious beliefs that are helpful or harmful to individuals but rather the possession of a spiritual belief system that seems to provide comfort and possibly answers to problems. Belonging to a spiritually involved community that provides validation for beliefs and nurturing when needed also seems to offer a positive psychological perspective. This does not mean that in order to be mentally healthy one needs to join a religious group, but it does suggest that nurturing one's spirituality (whether through religion or some other spiritual approach) and being a member of a spiritual community may provide opportunities to some people to give and receive support from others.

SUMMARY

Millions of Americans suffer from anxiety disorders, but only a small percentage of them are receiving the adequate treatment necessary to live normal lives. Billions of dollars are lost annually in productivity and disability with only minimal financial resources focused on actual medical and psychological treatments. Countless relationships, families, friendships, jobs, careers, goals, and interests are disturbed or lost due to undiagnosed or undertreated anxiety disorders. Primary care physicians and mental health professionals must be aware of the variety of symptom patterns frequently presented by groups differing by gender, age, culture, sexual orientation, and/or minority status. Early, accurate diagnoses and appropriate treatment or referrals to mental health professionals are essential to providing appropriate care.

3

Theories of Anxiety Disorders

Anxiety disorders are complex and complicated, involving different physical and psychological symptoms. There are a number of theories that offer a variety of explanations, and continuing research has led to new approaches, improved theories, and more effective treatments. While it may be tempting to consider which theory is the "correct" one, it is important to understand that no current single theory can explain everything about anxiety disorders. By examining some of the basic types of theories you will have a better understanding as to the nature of anxiety and anxiety disorders, what causes them, how they can be understood, and how they can be treated.

BIOLOGICAL THEORIES

Anxiety and panic attacks appear to be biologically and possibly genetically based since most of the symptoms are physical in nature, and anxiety disorders tend to run in families. Since a variety of medications are effective in treating anxiety, it seems to imply that the drug is "fixing" something at the biological level. However, it is not yet fully clear as to what all of these biological mechanisms may be. Some assert that genetic contributions play a significant role, while others have focused on the brain itself. Others have examined the role of various chemical "messengers" (neurotransmitters) in the central nervous system, and most of the prescribed medical treatments that are effective in treating anxiety disorders work by modifying the way these chemical messengers actually work. These "messengers" are chemicals that transmit information from one neuron (a type of brain cell) to another, and this is very important in understanding what happens in people's brains when they are dealing with anxiety or other psychological problems. This does not, however, mean that all psychological problems are "caused" by a chemical imbalance. When people become depressed or anxious, for example, these emotional states will also change the level of the neurotransmitters in the brain, which means that in this case the chemical imbalance is not the cause of the anxiety but is rather *caused by* the anxiety.

For decades, researchers have tried to unlock the genetic "secrets" in an effort to discover how genes may contribute to the development of anxiety disorders. Compelling evidence from a number of family studies demonstrates that people who have various specific types of an anxiety disorders are more likely to be related to someone who suffers from the same disorder. Other studies have shown that the presence of anxiety disorders in immediate family members and close relatives of anxiety disorder patients is very high. One of the challenges to understanding the role of genetics in anxiety disorders is that increased rates of psychological problems in family members of anxiety patients may also be due to the fact that they live in similar environments and have other comparable experiences.

Another way to study genetic factors is to look at twins. Identical twins (monozygotic) are exactly the same genetically, while fraternal twins (dizygotic) are no more genetically similar than any other brothers or sisters. Studying twin pairs where at least one of the twins has an anxiety disorder is one way to see how important genetics are in the development of anxiety disorders. One common criticism of these types of studies, however, is that twins tend to share an environment that is even more similar than their family members share, including non-twin siblings. Some twin studies have avoided this issue by studying twins who were raised together and twins who were raised separately due to a family situation that required them to be separated at birth or shortly thereafter. Most researchers have concluded that there is a higher rate of both twins having an anxiety disorder if they are identical rather than fraternal twins. While this certainly suggests some genetic influence, at least half of the identical twin pairs do not both have anxiety disorders when one twin does have the disorder. Thus, anxiety disorders may have some genetic component, but it is also true that genes *cannot* be the only determinant—there must be other things operating as well. Current research suggests that, rather than directly inheriting an anxiety disorder, people inherit the *predisposition* for developing one—this means that they are more likely to develop the disorder than someone without the genetic predisposition, but it is not guaranteed.

Recent research has also examined the role of certain structures in the central nervous system and how they relate to the development of anxiety, with much of the work focusing on the structures in the limbic system, which is sometimes called the "pleasure center" of the brain. However, this system is much more complex than just relating to pleasure; it has to do with the expression of other emotions and appears to coordinate some of the activities of the neurotransmitters that we discussed earlier. The more we learn about the brain, its structures, and how they work, the clearer it becomes that the brain is at least part of what is relevant to the development of anxiety disorders.

Considering all of the information regarding genetics, brain structures, and neurotransmitters, it is tempting to conclude that problems with anxiety are due to underlying biological factors and that the best way to treat anxiety disorders is use of medication or other medical treatments. However, there is substantial research that supports alternative theories, and anxiety is not as simple as too much or too little of certain chemicals in the brain. Genetic factors may be involved in some, but not all, cases of anxiety disorder, and in others certain brain systems or processes may be responsible.

Many anxiety disorders are associated with self-reported symptoms of insomnia and fatigue. Sleep is one of the phenomena that is affected by both physiological and psychological factors, and people with anxiety disorders often suffer from insomnia (difficulty sleeping at night). The psychological and physiological mechanisms related to anxiety disorders and insomnia are not fully understood, but it is such a common occurrence that most clinicians who work with anxiety disorder patients find that they must also help them deal with sleep issues.

PSYCHOLOGICAL THEORIES

In addition to biological models, there are a number of psychological approaches that help us to understand anxiety disorders. *Psychodynamic* theorists look at a person's experiences in early life that are recorded in the subconscious mind as the primary causes of anxiety. Freud's theory called "psychoanalysis" dates back about a century and is certainly the most well known and influential psychodynamic theory.

Freud's theory of anxiety is based on the concept of fear of being overwhelmed by unconscious forces over which we feel we have no control.

This fear of overstimulation is the basis of all anxiety, according to Freud. He postulated three basic types of anxiety: *reality anxiety*, which we call *fear*, is based on a realistic threat in the environment. Here we first assess and then conclude that there is a realistic possibility of environmental factors overwhelming us with undesirable stimuli. For example, if we are walking through the woods and see a bear running toward us, we will experience the fear (reality anxiety) of overstimulation (being mauled or bitten) by the bear.

Neurotic anxiety is based on a fear of being overwhelmed by unacceptable sexual and aggressive impulses that demand fulfillment. However, since these impulses are inconsistent with our values and conscience, this will create the fear of what might happen if these unacceptable impulses were allowed expression. Freud also postulated *moral anxiety*, the fear that is produced when a person does, thinks, or imagines something that violates the standards of the conscience, which is generally referred to as *guilt*. According to Freud, anxiety is a signal to the ego (or core of the self) of impending overstimulation by realistic fears, unacceptable impulses, or by thoughts and behaviors that may lead us into trouble by violating the rules of the conscience.

Most of Freud's writings about neuroses address how people develop anxiety disorders, how they deal with it, and how it can be treated. Freud used the word "neurosis" to refer to anxiety disorders and other similar problems. Following Freud, other psychodynamic theorists have focused more upon mental processes like thinking and less on the instinctual and subconscious basis of anxiety. These other theorists also looked at child-hood experiences as the primary source of mental conflict that results in anxiety, but they also consider the adult experiences and problems rather than just focusing on childhood as the main source of anxiety.

Humanistic and *existential* theorists have developed different ideas about the origin of anxiety, and, while they are somewhat similar to the psycho-dynamic theorists and focus on what is inside a person's mind, they are less concerned about the subconscious basis of personality functioning and focus more upon the conscious mind and more immediate conflicts and problems. The humanistic theorists were mostly in vogue during the 1960s and 1970s, although philosophers and social theorists had written about humanistic approaches to understanding human behavior prior to and since that time.

The humanistic approach deviates from the strictly deterministic and the more historically prominent theoretical models: the psychodynamic and behavioral theories. The deterministic models assert that all behavior is caused by knowable factors, and such things as free will are just an illusion.

The humanists assert that human beings are more than a collection of unconscious impulses or learned behaviors and that by only digging into an individual's unconscious processes we miss the humanity and richness of the human experience. Similarly, they believe that the behavioral theory that asserts that all behavior is the result of learning is misguided as well. If a strictly deterministic approach to human behavior is followed, as with psychodynamic and behavioral theorists, then human factors such as choice and free will do not fit. The humanists feel strongly that trying to understand behavior by reducing it to simple instincts and learned behaviors does not do justice to the complexity of the human experience, thoughts, feelings, and actions.

The humanistic theorists believe that all people are basically good and healthy, and it is only when people are exposed to environments that are not consistent with what is good and important to the individual that problems like anxiety emerge. When we have to adapt to unhealthy situations, we begin to experience problems. Consequently, treatment from a humanistic therapist involves providing a safe and accepting situation where people can feel free to express themselves and find ways to be true to who they really are and what they truly need to be a healthy and mature individual.

Similar to the humanistic theories, the existential approach was popular a few decades ago. During the period between World War I and World War II, several European psychiatrists became dissatisfied with traditional psychoanalysis and began to consider existentialism, a branch of philosophy that included a new model for understanding human personality and experience. They drew from the existential philosophers, plus a number of influential psychologists and psychiatrists. The existential theorists share many ideas with the humanists, although they tend to place more emphasis on the importance of choice and responsibility, as well as the vital necessity of free will. They are concerned with people making decisions in their own best interests and being "true to themselves." They believe that the basis of anxiety is "inauthenticity," which simply means that we are not being true to ourselves and that our behavior is not consistent with what is best and healthiest for us. However, the existential theorists differ from the humanists since they do not consider psychopathology (abnormal psychology) an illness. They view it as an experience that results from the choices one makes throughout life and that one of those choices is to continue feeling anxious.

The *behavioral* and *cognitive* theorists offer a very different approach to understanding anxiety. While the behavioral theories have held a prominent position in the psychological models of psychopathology for about a century, some of the newer cognitive and cognitive-behavioral models are more inclusive of a broader variety of psychological factors and are not as narrow and restrictive as the earlier behavioral models. The earliest works of the behaviorists, dealing with the development of anxiety, dates back to Watson and Rayner when in 1920 they demonstrated that a learned fear reaction could be taught to a youngster, "Little Albert," by using conditioning procedures. As an 18-month-old toddler, Albert was exposed to a white rat, which did not bother or concern him much. Then, while in the presence of the white rat Watson made a loud noise, which startled Albert and made him cry. From that moment forward, Albert was frightened of the white rat. Thus, Watson and Rayner reported that a phobia could be acquired through conditioning. Today, of course, this type of study would be considered unethical and not be permitted. However, during Watson's era there were no rules or limitations and, although some were very upset and concerned about his research methods, he had not violated any laws or standards of the time. From this somewhat questionable beginning, many researchers and theorists have pursued the idea that abnormal behavior, just as normal behavior, can be acquired through learning and conditioning and can be treated using the same types of learning approaches.

There appear to be a number of different ways in which people can "learn" to develop anxiety. *Classical conditioning* is the type of process that was responsible for Little Albert's acquired fear of rats. In this type of learning a particular stimulus is paired with a specific behavior, and after the new conditioned response is learned then the stimulus will produce the response. Like Little Albert, this appears to be the way many people develop phobias—they learn to be anxious in the presence of a specific stimulus (a phobic object—e.g., spiders or bugs).

Watson and others tried to assert that classical conditioning could account for the development of different psychological disorders, but it was clear that this model was too limited. Based primarily on the research of behavioral psychologist B. F. Skinner, a new model of learning emerged: *operant conditioning*. With this approach no evoking stimulus is required, and it is based on the idea that behavior can be shaped by its consequences. The fundamental concept in operant conditioning is that reinforcement, which refers to what happens following a response, increases the probability that the response will occur again. *Positive reinforcement* means that a response is more likely to occur when a positive consequence is introduced following a specific behavior. This is much like a reward—if you want someone to continue doing something, you reward them with something positive. You can also introduce *negative reinforcement*, which involves the removal of a negative outcome—this too would reinforce behavior. For example, I could reinforce a particular behavior in a labora-tory rat by giving it a food pellet for responding correctly (positive rein-forcement), or I could turn off a painful shock when it responded correctly (negative reinforcement). In both cases I have increased the probability of the correct response occurring again. Likewise, by removing the posi-tive reinforcer (or not removing a negative reinforcer) you can discourage the behavior that you want to reduce or eliminate, and it will cease in the absence of a reinforcer (extinction); or by adding a negative outcome or removing a positive one, you can directly punish the response. As it turns out, punishment is not usually a reliable way to change behavior, but reinforcement or extinction is more effective. This does not mean that punishment can never be used to change behavior, however, the use of reinforcement or extinction when possible is more efficient and more effective. The behavioral approaches in general have provided some very good ways of treating abnormal behavior like anxiety, and many of these treatments have proven to be very effective.

Another approach to learning and behavioral models demonstrates convincingly that during *observational learning* people can acquire com-plex behaviors by simply observing another person's behavior. Observa-tional learning appears to occur cognitively (in the person's mind) and does not require the person to perform the behavior themselves in order to learn. It also helps to explain the acquisition of complex behavior, including certain types of anxiety responses. Although this theory is grounded in the operant conditioning heritage, it was one of the first modern theories to incorporate cognitive factors into a learning model, and this set the stage for the newer cognitive and cognitive behavioral models that were to follow.

Although influential, the learning and conditioning methods are not adequate to explain the variety of acquired fears or the reasons that some stimuli are more likely to lead to phobic reactions than others. Some feel that there are biological factors that determine when some fears form and others do not. In fact, some theorists feel that certain fears have an evolu-tionary basis. For example, being afraid of snakes, heights, the dark, etc. may actually have some survival basis and, thus, may have been passed on either genetically or through cultural channels.

Other researchers have found that some people are more prone to develop fear reactions to some stimuli and that selective exposure to spe-cific types of experiences during development is more likely to lead to an increase of phobias. Further, some children tend to be more shy and with-drawn, and this may be a factor in the later development of social phobia and other anxiety disorders. Other findings establish that when compared to nonanxious individuals, people with social phobia remember their parents discouraging them from socializing, placing undue importance on the opinions of others, and using shame as a means of discipline. They also found other predictors of social phobia such as a childhood history of separation anxiety or self-consciousness or shyness, and that these young-sters reported more shyness and a lower frequency of dating during adoles-cence. Another factor in the development of social phobia is *perfectionism* because the fear of making mistakes, especially in the presence of others, is a major issue with this disorder.

COGNITIVE THEORIES

Conditioning and learning are important to understanding anxiety disor-ders, but they are not adequate explanations for the full range of factors related to anxiety. A more recent approach comes from the cognitive theorists, which focuses on attention, perception, and thinking, and how these processes affect the development and/or maintenance of anxiety. George Kelly, in the 1950s and 1960s, was one of the first to take the cognitive perspective further into the understanding of how mental processes are relevant to human personality and abnormal behavior. His approach is called *personal construct theory*, and it studies the ways in which people think about and anticipate events in their lives. He felt that people use *constructs* to understand and anticipate the world, that is, to make sense of it. These constructs are cognitive structures that help us to organize information and ideas into coherent wholes that allow us to think and anticipate efficiently.

Albert Ellis was one of the first psychologists to effectively build an entire approach to psychotherapy based upon cognitive techniques, and his ideas were quickly incorporated into therapeutic methods and train-ing. His approach, *rational-emotive psychotherapy*, was influential during the 1960s and 1970s, and there are still therapists who use his approach, although few identify themselves primarily as rational-emotive therapists. Ellis's ideas have significantly influenced the manner in which therapists work today and have helped to identify some of the dysfunctional ways people think about things and how to confront and change their thinking patterns.

More recently, Beck and Emery began applying some new cognitive approaches to the understanding and treatment of anxiety. Originally, Aaron Beck applied his cognitive approach to depression, which has been a helpful and positive contribution to the understanding and treatment of this disorder. Then shifting their ideas and approaches to anxiety disorders, they applied some of Kelly's ideas about the development of constructs (ways of organizing information) to the development of anxiety. These constructs relate to the concepts of danger and vulnerability and to the person's estimation of their ability to cope with the danger.

Another recent cognitive model of anxiety is the *fear of fear* approach. Goldstein and Chambliss suggest that following a panic attack people may learn to fear that any change in their physical state might indicate the possibility of another panic attack. Thus, even low-level physical sensations become a conditioned stimulus that triggers fear and worry. Some researchers have pointed out that the fear of anxiety itself arises from the association of internal cues with panic attacks. Although this model relies on cognitive factors, it also employs physiological and behavioral elements. However, the fear of fear concept is the central notion and depends upon beliefs about anxiety, danger, and vulnerability. The cognitive portion relates to the ways people think about minor physical changes or about the risks they fear, which are present in response to the *possibility* that they might experience feelings of anxiety. This often results in an overreaction to minor physical changes and mentally exaggerating the dangers and risks that they now associate with anxiety.

Reiss and McNally developed a similar model called the *anxiety sensitivity model*, which is based on the notion that some people believe that experiencing anxiety can cause illness, embarrassment, or additional anxiety and leads to more significant problems. While this is an extension of the fear of fear model, it rests on the assumption that the belief structure is the fundamental reason why anxiety becomes more intense and problematic for some people.

Most of the cognitive models are based on the idea that people with anxiety disorders are selectively sensitive to information that will stimulate and continue their anxiety. Thus, they tend to pay more attention to things that they are fearful of, and they also give that information more importance than it actually deserves. Thus, things that they fear are things that they notice and think about frequently, and when they feel as though these things are a threat to them they will exaggerate the threat. Thus, their anxiety response may feel reasonable to them, but in reality the anxiety is an exaggerated response if we logically evaluate the actual risk. Of course, treating an anxiety disorder is never as simple as logically explaining to a person that their fear is irrational—in their mind it is perfectly understandable as to why they are so upset. Remember, these are emotional problems, not logical problems, and we will not solve them with rational explanation.

Although the cognitive approaches have been beneficial in the development of theories and treatments for anxiety disorders, they have limitations as well. Theorists refer to *cognitive predispositions* for dealing with certain types of information in specific ways called *schemata* (singular is a *schema*). These cognitive schemata might function to elicit anxiety responses in some people. However, if the cognitive schemata are the triggering mechanisms for anxiety, where do they come from? Since they must be either acquired or already inside the person, they are either learned by the person through their experiences or are part of the biological system and "hard-wired" into the brain. In either case, this aspect of the cognitive model depends upon another and different type of model (e.g., either learning or biological) in order to actually explain why cognitions lead to anxiety.

The conclusion that can be drawn from these findings is that cognitive factors are an important contribution to the understanding and treatment of anxiety disorders. However, it is obvious that cognitive factors alone do not explain everything about the causes of anxiety and that, as helpful as they are, we must rely on other factors in order to make sense of the complex world of anxiety. Of course, as mentioned above, no single theory or type of theory can explain all of the aspects of anxiety and anxiety disorders. To the extent that we can integrate elements of all of the theories, we have a better chance of understanding and explaining how anxiety works and how it can actually become a disorder.

WHO IS VULNERABLE?

One line of inquiry has examined issues of patient vulnerability, focusing on various factors that make people more susceptible to anxiety disorders and on how to prevent, minimize, and treat them. This involves trying to understand the conditions or characteristics that might predispose a person to develop an anxiety disorder.

Some predisposing factors may be biological in nature, and in many studies of nonhuman animals they have found significant differences between animals from the same species (e.g., monkeys) in how fearful and timid the individuals might be—some being very fearful and some very bold, for example. While these subjects are not human, additional research found several factors related to shyness and social fearfulness in human children that emerge very early and are consistent through childhood and adolescence. These behaviors include clinging to mother, crying easily, and a reluctance to interact with others—behaviors that are very anxiety-like. One difficulty is that children often cannot identify the emotions they are experiencing and, even after looking at anxiety-provoking stimulus pictures, some children still did not identify themselves as being anxious, although they showed higher levels of physical arousal. There are also psychological traits (e.g., introversion, activity level, startle response, etc.) that may relate to the later development of anxiety, and these, too, are stable throughout childhood and adolescence.

Researchers have explored additional physical factors that can affect someone's vulnerability for developing anxiety disorder. For example, some heart conditions are more likely to create feelings of anxiety, especially after the patient has been treated for a heart attack. Also, problems with the inner ear may make people somewhat light-headed and dizzy, and these symptoms often tend to make people more anxious.

Sleep is another factor that affects our vulnerability to developing anxiety disorders. Many studies have demonstrated that children, adolescents, and adults with anxiety disorders are more likely to have problems sleeping, and these difficulties often last for years. As discussed earlier, it does seem that the sleep disorders are usually the result of anxiety rather than the cause of it, but the sleep problems can also be a factor that indicates that the person is vulnerable to developing an anxiety disorder.

A very interesting line of research has examined some of the physical factors in the brain that may make some children more vulnerable to developing anxiety problems, particularly if paired with childhood trauma or abuse; these children are at high risk for developing an anxiety disorder. Once again, this suggests that in many people it is the combination of a physical and/or psychological factor and a specific type of environmental event or condition that will make these vulnerabilities actually result in a disorder.

SUMMARY

Many factors are involved in the causes of anxiety disorders, ranging from biological and psychological to social and cultural. No simple model of anxiety exists, but recent studies and theories have helped us to understand and to treat anxiety disorders more effectively. Continued research will offer new and improved treatments, and we know that those with anxiety disorders who receive adequate treatment will typically improve.

4

❖

Types of Anxiety Disorders I: Generalized Anxiety Disorder and Panic Disorder

Each type of anxiety disorder has its own distinctive symptoms, problems, and specific types of treatments. Those with anxiety disorders often have comorbid conditions (physical or psychological conditions that are co-existing), which can frequently confuse the diagnostic picture and complicate treatment and recovery. Two of the more common anxiety disorders are generalized anxiety disorder and panic disorder. As different as these disorders sound they are similar in that both are characterized by anxiety, and this anxiety is severe enough to significantly impair the person's ability to function normally. However, the manifestation of the anxiety is clearly different and the types of treatments that are used may differ as well, depending on the patient and his or her symptoms.

GENERALIZED ANXIETY DISORDER (GAD)

GAD is characterized by extensive and continuous feelings of anxiety and/or excessive worrying. Since it frequently coexists with other conditions, some professionals have questioned if it is an independent disorder or if it always exists as part of another problem. Professionals often miss diagnosing patients with GAD because the symptoms are not recognized as a separate problem. Past research has rarely focused on GAD since some of the diagnostic criteria have changed, and there have been some studies where mental health professionals have disagreed about this diagnosis—some even feel that it should not be considered to be a separate and independent disorder. Today most professionals still consider GAD an acceptable diagnostic category, and in recent years progress has led to further understanding and improved treatment options for people diagnosed with GAD. About 1.6 percent of the general population suffers from GAD, and the lifetime prevalence rate is 5.1 percent, which means that over the span of a life over 5 percent of people will suffer from GAD at some point. Although a relatively high percentage of people experience this common disorder, it does not receive as much attention as panic disorder. Interestingly, GAD is commonly diagnosed and treated in primary care settings (your family doctor's office) with 22 percent of patients complaining of anxiety problems. However, it is one of the least common disorders being treated in mental health centers, which implies that those with GAD are either not referred to mental health professionals or when they are, a different condition is diagnosed as the primary issue.

GAD is found more often in women and in midlife and older patients and less frequently diagnosed in adolescents and younger adults. GAD results in a significant number of disability days (similar to depression) and is often comorbid with depression, making the disability burden even higher. Appropriate diagnosis and use of psychological and medical treatments not only will reduce the frequency of GAD but will help to prevent comorbid major depression, which may accompany GAD or arise after GAD emerges.

GAD is characterized by excessive, recurrent, and prolonged worry and anxiety over simple daily concerns and minor issues. Typically, the focus of the anxiety shifts from one issue to another, unlike phobias where the source(s) of anxiety remains consistent. Patients are usually aware that their concerns are exaggerated and sometimes ridiculous, but they are not able to change how they feel or think. The daily anxiety is so prominent that it interferes with concentration, attention, short-term memory, decision making, and confidence—people do not trust themselves to do what they need to do in their daily lives. It becomes impossible to conduct normal activities such as work, school, socializing with family/friends, or maintaining significant relationships. Those who live with GAD continuously over a long period of time begin to "get used to" feeling anxious, but they also feel that there is nothing they can do to change it. Unfortunately, people with GAD often turn to alcohol or drugs to mask or manage their anxiety, and it may be the substance abuse that brings them initially into professional treatment.

According to the *Diagnostic and Statistical Manual*, a diagnosis of GAD requires the following criteria:

1. Excessive anxiety and worry occurring most days over a continuous six-month period, and it involves a number of events or activities.
2. The person feels that they cannot control the worry.
3. Anxiety and worry are associated with at least three of the following (only one for children):
    a. Restlessness or feeling "keyed up" or on edge
    b. Easily fatigued
    c. Difficulty concentrating or feeling like their mind just goes blank
    d. Irritability
    e. Muscle tension
    f. Sleep disturbances
4. Anxiety or worry is not confined to another clinical disorder.
5. Symptoms cause significant distress or impairment in social, work, or other important area of functioning.
6. Disturbance is not due to direct impact of a substance or a medical condition, and does not occur exclusively during a mood disorder, psychotic disorder, or other psychological disorder.

Although everyone occasionally feels anxious, specific criteria separate "normal" anxiety from GAD with the primary difference being extreme distress and clear impairment in normal functioning found in GAD patients. More recent approaches to understanding GAD have led to a major revision in the way we view GAD, and that is to focus on *worry* as the primary defining quality. In addition to worrying about many different things, people with GAD can worry about worrying or even worry about not worrying! Some people will worry almost superstitiously, as if worrying will prevent the feared outcomes from happening. GAD patients worry about family, personal finances, work, illness, and even minor things such as small mistakes or a social blunder, and most will report that they typically worry at least half of every single day. Children and teens are more likely to worry about school performance or performance in other areas like sports, music, or drama, although children and teens can worry obsessively about potentially catastrophic events like earthquakes, torna-does, asteroid strikes, etc. These youngsters seem to need excessive reas-surance about many things in their lives, including their own physical or mental imperfections and inadequacies. They are often perfectionists and frequently complain about multiple physical problems. Children and teens with GAD usually act quite mature, are serious and reserved, and are often the eldest in small, competitive, achievement-oriented families.

Most people with GAD will complain about cognitive difficulties such as attention, concentration, short-term memory, as well as troubling thoughts and worries and will typically manifest physical symptoms of anxiety like muscle tension (esp. in the neck and shoulders), headache (esp. in the front and back of the head), sweaty palms, feeling shaky, dryness of the mouth, pounding heart, and difficulty breathing. Many will report severe gastro-intestinal (GI) symptoms with about 30 percent having severe irritable bowel syndrome (IBS), which causes multiple digestive problems. Although chest pains are common in patients with panic disorder, they also exist in about 34 percent of GAD patients who do not suffer from panic attacks. Due to the myriad physical symptoms, GAD patients tend to undergo many physical and laboratory tests in order to rule out physical disorders and ailments, and will often have a high use of general medical services.

Frequently, GAD is found to coexist with other disorders including:

1. Strong association with major depressive disorder and dysthymia (a milder mood disorder)
2. Low association with panic disorder (PD)—someone could have both GAD and PD, but it is not common
3. Hypomania, one of the characteristics of bipolar II disorder
4. Higher risk for suicide attempts
5. Treated professionally more frequently and have more frequent work problems
6. Alcoholism, although not as common as in other anxiety disorders and the pattern of abuse is often brief and nonpersistent
7. When alcohol use disorder is present, GAD onset is later than the onset of alcohol use disorder

In summary, GAD is now considered a disorder of excessive and uncontrollable worry, a considerable shift from the earlier conceptualization that focused more on the physical aspects of GAD symptoms. Worry and difficulties with other cognitive processes now account for most of the symptoms that are identified as responsible for the cause and maintenance of this common and troubling disorder. Fortunately, great strides in the last twenty years have improved both the diagnosing and treatment of GAD.

Although most research reports a typical recovery rate of about 40 percent, GAD remains one of the most difficult anxiety disorders to treat even though it is a common, disabling, often chronic, and expensive condition. Due to the variety of symptoms, several different types of treatment are often required; especially for the physical symptoms. Anxiolytic (antianxiety) medications and physical treatments such as deep muscle relaxation, meditation, and massage are often helpful, although not usually curative. It is also very common for psychiatrists and other physicians to prescribe some of the newer antidepressants for GAD patients even though they may not be depressed. However, these drugs will often help the person deal more effectively with their anxiety. The most common and successful treatments today involve cognitive-behavioral therapies (CBT), which will often include the use of relaxation techniques to help reduce the amount and frequency of worrying, as well as many other CBT techniques. This type of therapy can, and often is, coupled with medication so that the patient is being treated with both types of therapy—medication and CBT.

Newly developed psychological treatments are emerging in the cognitive realm that address cognitive and behavioral symptoms. Patients with GAD often pay more attention to stimuli that imply some degree of threat over neutral stimuli when both are present, and clinically anxious people with GAD consistently pay more attention to things that they feel are threatening. Research has shown that GAD patients who are treated in a program designed to improve their attention span have been successful at decreasing the focus on threatening things and decreasing their anxiety symptoms over the course of treatment. This suggests that the treatment of GAD cannot simply attend to physical symptoms but must also focus on cognitive and behavioral symptoms, especially those most directly related to worry.

PANIC DISORDER (PD)

One of the most challenging and well known anxiety disorders is panic disorder (PD). People who suffer from panic attacks experience severe and frightening symptoms such as pounding heart, trouble breathing, dizziness, chest pains, and nausea, and usually report being in poorer physical health than the general population. One of the characteristics of people with PD is being frightened by their own physical symptoms, including the feeling that they are going to die or are going crazy. Panic attacks are the product of *catastrophically* misinterpreting physical arousal sensations that occur in the context of "normal" anxiety, as well as overreacting to

other sources of arousal such as physical illness, exercise, and the inges-
tion of certain substances. Experiencing an acute anxiety attack during or
in association with a real, actual physical threat is considered a fear reaction. This is not the same as experiencing a true panic attack, which
occurs in the absence of any real danger. Patients are rarely able to reliably
predict when a panic attack will occur, although there are occasions when
an attack may be expected and does occur. A panic attack can strike at
any time, even during sleep, and usually lasts about 15–30 minutes. The
symptoms will peak at about ten minutes, although some of the residual
symptoms may last longer. This unpredictability of an attack is quite
significant to patients, since the fear of having another attack can be disabling as well.

Anyone can experience a panic attack under the right circumstances,
but a diagnosis of panic disorder requires more than the occasional panic
attack and must meet specific diagnostic criteria. Most people who experience a panic attack will never go on to develop panic disorder. One study
found that the one-year prevalence rate for any type of panic attack
(either unexpected or situationally caused) was about 28 percent, which
means that over one quarter of the population will experience an anxiety
attack during a given year, but most of them will never develop panic
disorder.

Panic disorder occurs in six million Americans annually, affecting women
about twice as frequently as men, although the clinical features, such as
number and severity of symptoms, are much the same across the sexes. PD
often appears in late adolescence or young adulthood, and a genetic con-
nection gives relatives of PD patients a higher probability of developing it.
It does not mean, however, that if someone is diagnosed with panic disorder that their family members will develop it as well. More current models
of panic disorder focus on the "fear of anxiety" construct, suggesting that
there is a learning component to the disorder. In the expectancy model of
fear, panic attacks result from having the predisposition to grossly misin-
terpret and to respond with fear to normal sensations of arousal. This is
also complicated by patients possessing a learned fear of anxiety that is
continually maintained by their experiencing panic episodes. Some believe that this "vicious cycle" first begins with anything that can cause
arousal and then can lead to a misinterpretation of emerging physical
symptoms; second, anxiety emerges and accelerates to the point of panic;
and finally, the person learns to fear the original cause of arousal as well as
any other situations where a similar arousal might occur.

Panic disorder is diagnosed in about 10 percent of patients seen at mental health clinics and between 10–60 percent seen in various medical

specialty clinics (e.g., cardiology [heart] and pulmonology [lungs]). A number of studies have examined the lifetime prevalence rate of PD, and depending on the study these rates are between 1–3.5 percent. Generally, the prevalence rates are fairly consistent around the world. The age of onset of PD most frequently occurs within two age groups: between 15–19 years and 25–30 years. PD is rarely found in ages over 65 and as in younger samples, when it does occur it affects twice as many women as men.

The frequency of panic attacks varies considerably in individuals with panic disorder; those who experience repeated panic attacks can become disabled by restricting their activities and avoiding situations for fear of having a panic attack. As mentioned earlier, many people with PD suffer from agoraphobia, or the fear of being in unfamiliar or "unsafe" situations. In clinical samples, PD with agoraphobia is more common than PD without it. If panic disorder is diagnosed before agoraphobia develops, it is one of the most treatable anxiety disorders. However, people who go "doctor shopping," trying one doctor after another looking for an answer to their problems, will frequently delay getting appropriate treatment, and this will usually mean that treatment will take longer and be more involved.

In general, treatment for panic disorder usually involves medications in conjunction with psychotherapy in order to address the physical, cognitive, and behavioral symptoms of PD. One complicating factor is that PD is frequently comorbid with conditions like depression, drug abuse, or alcoholism. PD with or without agoraphobia is also associated with a poor overall quality of life, as well as impaired occupational, scholastic, and social functioning. But as a highly treatable condition, it is important to recognize, diagnose, and treat PD early and adequately. Without treatment, PD and agoraphobia may wax and wane, but they both appear to be chronic conditions if not treated.

A diagnosis of PD will specify whether it is with or without agoraphobia, otherwise the criteria are exactly the same. According to the *Diagnostic and Statistical Manual*, someone with PD will have at least four of the following symptoms:

1. Rapid heartbeat
2. Sweating
3. Shortness of breath
4. Choking feeling or sensation of being smothered
5. Dizziness
6. Nausea
7. Feelings of unreality
8. Numbness

9. Hot flashes or chills
10. Chest pain
11. Fear of dying
12. Fear of going insane

The diagnostic criteria for PD with agoraphobia are:

1. Both (a) and (b):
    a. Recurrent and unexpected panic attacks
    b. At least one of the attacks has been followed by one month or more of:
        i.   Persistent concern about having another attack
        ii. Worry about the implications of the attack or its consequences (e.g., losing control, having a heart attack, going crazy)
2. Presence of agoraphobia
3. Panic attacks are not a result of the direct physical effects of a substance (e.g., a drug of abuse or medication) or a general medical condition.
4. Panic attacks are not better accounted for by another mental disorder, including other anxiety disorders.

The diagnostic criteria for agoraphobia are:

1. Anxiety about being in places or situations from which escape might be difficult or embarrassing, or where help may not be available during a panic attack; usually fears different clusters of situations and venturing into them, with the number increasing over time.
2. Situations are avoided or endured with marked distress and worry about having a panic attack or similar symptoms. Confronting difficult situations is usually aided by the presence of a companion.
3. Anxiety or avoidance is not better accounted for by another mental disorder.

Interestingly, some patients do not experience a fearful response as a result of a panic attack. About 30 percent of panic attacks occur without the fear of dying or of going crazy, and they do not differ in terms of age, age of onset, or frequency from those who experience attacks with feelings of fear. Due to the lack of fear, the attacks are rarely associated with shortness of breath, trembling, feeling smothered, the feeling of being different and or not like themselves, and other physical symptoms. Patients who do not experience the same fears found in other PD patients are less likely to experience anxiety about having another panic attack or fears of being treated with medication, and they are less likely to develop agoraphobia or other clinical disorders such as major depression. However, these patients are frequently diagnosed and treated for PD just as the patients who are more fearful.

Risk factors for PD include gender—women are twice as likely to develop PD—and marital status; the highest lifetime rates for PD are widowed, separated, or divorced people (especially men). No consistent findings relate PD to educational level. Some have found a relationship between smoking and PD, but the causal link is unclear. Also, an understandable link between pulmonary disease and PD has been reported, which makes sense since experiencing breathing problems can frequently trigger a panic attack.

The most common of comorbid anxiety disorders that occur with PD (not including agoraphobia, since it is an element of the diagnosis) are: social phobia, GAD, obsessive-compulsive disorder (OCD), and posttraumatic stress disorder (PTSD). Between 30–60 percent of patients with PD will also suffer from a depressive disorder and about 36 percent will suffer from substance abuse, using alcohol or drugs to self-medicate the anxiety symptoms, although recent evidence suggests that substance abuse usually begins prior to the development of panic disorder. Some studies demonstrate that major depressive disorder occurs in up to 56 percent of patients with PD at some point in their life, and in approximately two-thirds of these cases, the symptoms of depression develop along with or following the PD. However, since major depression often precedes PD, it cannot be assumed that the depression is always a reaction to PD. Medical conditions that are likely to be comorbid with PD include cardiac, gastrointestinal, respiratory, and neurological diseases.

Experiencing a panic attack is terrifying and is a primary reason that people seek emergency department consultations. Frequent emergency room visits are one of the reasons why PD sufferers generate high medical expenses, coupled with costly medical tests, to rule out other medical problems. PD is also a leading cause for people seeking mental health services, surpassing both schizophrenia and mood disorders. Typically, people with PD do not begin their search for help by contacting mental health professionals but are referred by a physician who has no medical explanation for the patient's symptoms.

Seasonal and meteorological changes affect people with PD similarly to those with seasonal affective disorder (SAD). The frequency of panic attacks varies by month, usually increasing in August and December;

although, if a patient peaks in August, they typically will not increase in December and vice versa. Panic attacks are also more likely to occur during cloudy weather, during hot or cold extremes, and when it is humid. There are no clear and agreed-upon reasons why weather would affect PD, but research continues to examine the effects of weather and barometric pressure changes on psychological and emotional functioning.

Although PD is a highly treatable condition, especially if caught early, it is not often recognized and diagnosed accurately in the primary care setting, which can lead to unnecessary and costly diagnostic procedures, as well as inappropriate referrals to cardiologists. In one study, medical specialists were given a survey to determine their knowledge of panic attacks and the availability of effective treatments. Unfortunately, many physicians were not very familiar with the symptoms and treatments for PD. In fact, many did not know that the first line treatment for PD is psychological treatment (e.g., cognitive-behavioral therapy), which is one reason why primary care physicians simply prescribe medication rather than refer the patient to a mental health professional. One risk of just using medication is that if the person discontinues the medication or if the medication is not working well, the symptoms will return. Another risk is that most patients with PD have other comorbid psychological and physical disorders, which means that prescribing medication is complex. These patients need to be referred to a psychiatrist or other specialist who deals with psychiatric medications. Typical treatments for PD include medication, but this is rarely adequate by itself and must be coupled with other types of psychological treatments. Cognitive-behavioral therapy is the approach that receives the most support as it offers a variety of behavioral and cognitive strategies to minimize the symptoms of panic.

New types of treatment are being introduced and evaluated, including panic-focused psychodynamic psychotherapy (PFPP), which is based on older forms of treatment dating back to Freud's psychoanalysis. However, since the older psychodynamic approaches often take longer and are difficult to evaluate, they are rarely used. More recent and briefer forms of psychodynamic treatments such as PFPP are being employed and are proving effective in treating PD.

Identifying what triggers panic attacks is of primary importance, although the actual cause of a panic attack is rarely found within the immediate situation but rather in the accumulation of many factors over time. In response to the question, "What caused my panic attack?" the real answer is usually, "All of the above." Unfortunately, people suffering from PD would like a simple answer for the cause and what to do to make it go away. However, the causes, the symptoms, and the treatment for this complex disorder are often unclear and confusing to people who are not specialists or researchers.

Whether a person is diagnosed with PD or experiences an isolated panic attack, it is important to remember that the panic attack itself does not pose any real physical danger—although the person experiencing such an attack would find that difficult to believe. While suffering a panic attack, people need to mentally accept the fact that it is indeed occurring and try not to fight the symptoms; it will usually subside within 10–20 minutes. It is very difficult for someone who is in the midst of a panic attack to think rationally, but if they can ride it out rather than become more upset, the panic attack will subside more quickly. It is also important to recognize the early warning signs of a panic attack because practicing some effective techniques (e.g., regulated breathing) can actually stop or minimize the attack. Sometimes people can abruptly tell themselves, "Stop it," and immediately focus on something other than themselves as a means of shortening or lessening the impact of an attack—this works best if you recognize it early. Finally, if someone experiences four or more attacks during a month and/or the fear of having another attack becomes disruptive to one's life, it is necessary to seek professional help from a specialist who is experienced in treating PD.

SUMMARY

The two types of anxiety disorders discussed in this chapter, GAD and PD, involve different symptom patterns and are treated with different techniques and methods. GAD is characterized by lower levels of and more diffuse types of anxiety and worry that emerge in varying degrees most of the time and on most days. PD involves acute and intense periods of anxiety that do not last long but are frightening and can be incapacitating. The fear of future panic attacks can severely limit activities and the quality of life for patients. These two anxiety disorders share similarities as well and are both characterized by anxiety, although the type of anxiety experienced is generally quite different. Most importantly, both conditions respond well to medications and psychotherapies, especially when diagnosed and treated early. It is critical that providers at the primary care level where these disorders are typically first seen understand and recognize the symptoms of GAD and PD and make the appropriate referrals in a timely manner. One of the most frustrating times for professionals is seeing a patient with GAD or PD who is not able or willing to access effective treatments. Improving the education of patients about available treatments and of informing medical professionals about how to recognize these disorders and to refer patients to the appropriate specialists will increase the chances that all patients have access to appropriate care when they need it.

5

❖

Types of Anxiety Disorders II: Phobias and Obsessive-Compulsive Disorder

In addition to generalized anxiety disorder and panic disorder, there are several other anxiety-based conditions that include specific and social phobias, posttraumatic stress disorder (PTSD) and acute stress disorder (ASD), and obsessive-compulsive disorder (OCD). These disorders differ from generalized anxiety disorder (GAD) and panic disorder (PD) but, unquestionably, involve and are identified with anxiety. This chapter will focus on phobias and obsessive-compulsive disorder, and we will deal with PTSD and ASD in the next chapter.

PHOBIAS

Phobia is the most identifiable and understandable of the anxiety disorders when it involves common fears such as snakes or dangerous animals. However, other feared objects or situations that do not seem to be an obvious threat may still be true phobias. Phobias appear to be learned fear reactions that develop and are maintained by understandable psychological processes. A fear is learned when a neutral object becomes the source of a phobia through a learning process called "classical conditioning" where the stimulus (phobic object) is linked to the fear response. This is then followed by avoidance learning, which occurs when a person is in an anxious situation where they are forced to confront a phobic object and then run away or find some way to avoid the feared object. When they avoid the phobic object this will decrease the anxiety, which is more comfortable, and so it is as if they are rewarding themselves for avoiding the thing/situation they are afraid of. Of course, if someone is rewarded for avoiding something (by reducing anxiety), they are now more likely to avoid this feared object in the future, which is how phobias are learned and maintained. This type of avoidance learning is called "operant conditioning," where learning occurs by shaping behavior through the consequences of behavior (e.g., rewards or punishments).

Mild fears of certain objects are not unusual or pathological, but irrational or disproportionate fears warrant a diagnosis of phobia, particularly when the fear causes significant distress and/or impairs the person socially, occupationally, or educationally. Children will pass through different developmental stages that often include being fearful of various things, but most will gradually outgrow their fears without any problems. Some childhood fears can continue into adulthood and, occasionally, become diagnostically relevant. To qualify for the diagnosis of phobia, there must be a *persistent, irrational fear* and *avoidance* of the specific thing or activity that elicits the fear. Further, the diagnosis is only offered when the phobia impairs the individual's social, occupational, educational, or other important functioning.

Generally, phobias are listed in three groups: agoraphobia, specific phobia, and social phobia. Agoraphobia, the fear of going out to new or different places, was discussed in Chapter 4 in relation to panic disorder. Specific phobias are common and rarely require treatment, as they seldom significantly disrupt a person's life. Common types of specific phobias often involve animals like spiders, snakes, mice, rats, and dogs. Other types of phobias include fear of flying, heights, injections, public transportation, confined spaces, dentists, storms, tunnels, and bridges. Although some of these fears can be disruptive, it is a testimony to a person's creativity as to how they can avoid the objects they fear and still manage to function normally. Famous sports announcer John Madden is afraid to fly, so he travels around the country in a huge, luxurious motor home. The last major type of phobia is social phobia, which includes generalized social phobia and specific (or discrete) social phobia. In both cases the person becomes severely anxious while in general or specific types of social situations.

SPECIFIC PHOBIAS

Phobias are among the most common mental disorders, and there is a lifetime prevalence of 11.25 percent for specific phobias and 2.73 percent for social phobia. It is estimated that about 19.2 million American adults suffer from some type of phobia, with women being affected about twice as frequently for specific phobias as are men. This is particularly true of animal phobias, although there are fewer differences between the sexes for acrophobia (fear of heights) and trypanophobia (fear of blood and/or injections). Typically, phobias emerge in childhood or adolescence and persist into adulthood, but they are not the same as normal, developmental childhood fears that usually just go away. Also, phobias tend to run in families and are assumed to be the result of observational or other forms of learning.

Specific phobias are usually very specific, persistent, and unreasonable fears of a particular object or situation and are the second most common anxiety disorder after social phobia. Although they tend to be less incapacitating than other anxiety disorders, the person usually recognizes the fear as unrealistic and most are able to adjust their lifestyles in order to completely avoid or at least minimize contact with the feared object. Some intense phobias are so specific that the person can perform certain tasks in situations that seem potentially fear producing but do not seem to result in the phobic response. For example, trained pilots with severe fear of heights are often unable to climb a stepladder but have no problem flying a plane; or athletes who ski the highest mountains can't look off the side of a bridge. While this may seem irrational, remember that the very nature of a phobia is a fear that is irrational. In most if not all anxiety disorders the fear of a loss of control is often included with feelings of anxiety and that seems to explain this apparent paradox when people with phobias can face some situations where one might think they would be fearful. Pilots have control of their plane and skiers are in control of themselves as they head down a slope; therefore, they do not notice the heights while they are performing because they feel totally in control of the situation.

A person with a genuine phobia who is forced to face the feared object or situation will usually experience acute anxiety and even a panic attack. However, if affected people seldom encounter the feared object (e.g., snakes), they may not bother to pursue treatment since the phobia does not adversely affect their daily lives. It is encouraging to note that treatment for phobias is usually successful, and specific phobias respond very well to psychotherapies that focus on the fears and the ways to reduce them. Interestingly, many people with specific phobia are fearful of more than one thing, although this does not seem to complicate either the understanding of or the treatment of phobias.

SOCIAL PHOBIA

Social phobia is a common problem that is frequently underdiagnosed and undertreated. It may emerge as a generalized type of phobia, where people are fearful in most social situations, or the nongeneralized type (usually called discrete or specific social phobia), which focuses on only one or two situations that are usually related to public performance of some kind (e.g., stage fright or fear of public speaking). Social phobia affects about 15 million American adults (6.8 percent of the population). It produces undue embarrassment and anxiety in social situations and is extreme enough to impair normal social functioning. In this particular type of phobia, women tend to predominate, but not by much. Men are more fearful than women of urinating in public bathrooms and of returning items to a store, whereas women are more fearful of talking to people in authority, public speaking, being the center of attention, expressing disagreement, and throwing a party.

People with social phobia are extremely self-conscious when in social situations, fear being watched and judged by others, and fear doing something embarrassing. They may worry and obsess for days or weeks prior to doing something social even though they are aware that their fears are unrealistic and unreasonable. Even if they succeed at doing something that they fear, they will worry excessively before the event, be nervous during it, and then worry for hours following it about what they did, how they did, and how people may have judged them. Even if they are successful at their social task, they will still be fearful the next time.

Social phobia can be limited to one or a few situations or generalized to any social situation, but it is most definitely an anxiety condition that displays many of the physical symptoms of anxiety. It usually emerges in childhood or adolescence and persists into adulthood. Some have proposed that a genetic factor is involved, but this is still unclear and the mechanisms of action are not well understood. Social phobia tends to run in families, a rate that is three times higher in patients' families than in the general population. While observational learning and other learning processes may be responsible, a higher concordance (both twins have the disorder) of social phobia in monozygotic (identical) than dizygotic (fraternal) twins implies a genetic process at least in part. However, even if there is a genetic tendency to develop social phobia, it is still acquired by learning—it just may be that some people may be more likely to learn the phobic response than others.

Questions about the relationship between shyness and social phobia persist, but they are not the same issues at all. One study looked at shy people with and without social phobia, as well as non-shy people with and without social phobia. In both the shy and non-shy groups, people with social phobia reported more symptomatology, more functional impairment, and a lower quality of life than those without social phobia. About one-third of highly shy people without social phobia reported no social fears at all. Both shy people without social phobia and socially phobic subjects reported similar levels of anxiety in normal conversation, but the socially phobic group reported more anxiety during the task of giving a speech, and the social phobia subjects performed less effectively than those without social phobia across all tasks. Clearly, social phobia is not just a severe case of shyness.

The anxiety associated with social phobia can be so intense that it may lead to physical reactions like blushing, stammering, sweating, gastro-intestinal upset, racing heart, trembling limbs, and even a full-scale panic attack. These physical symptoms can evoke intense emotions that are hidden most of the time, and the physical reactions that are experienced often produce additional embarrassment and humiliation. One of the main challenges is the intrusive nature of the symptoms, which can interfere with important areas of a person's functioning. For example, in one music school 16 percent of the students said that performance anxiety had limited their careers, and at an international conference of symphony and opera musicians, 24 percent said that they had suffered seriously from stage fright.

Social phobia is a common diagnosis that may affect from 1–13 percent of the population, depending on how the phobia is defined. If we look at the most serious variants of this disorder, it is more likely that about 1–2 percent of the population experiences significant impairment of work and/or social life. During one phone survey 21 percent of the respondents said that they try to avoid public speaking and 17 percent said that they try to avoid eating in a restaurant; another 3 percent try to avoid writing in public, and 0.2 percent said they consistently avoid urinating in public restrooms.

In terms of comorbidities, social phobia frequently co-occurs with other disorders: 59 percent of patients with social phobia also had another specific phobia, 49 percent had panic disorder with agoraphobia, 19 percent were alcohol abusers (often self-medicating to reduce the anxiety), 17 percent suffered from major depressive disorder, and 10–20 percent of people in clinics for treatment of anxiety disorders also had social phobia, the most common diagnosis for a person with another anxiety disorder. Major depression is often associated with social phobia, and family members of patients with social phobia also experience a high rate of depression. Alcoholics are more likely to have social phobia and may use alcohol to "self-medicate" their anxiety. Another interesting observation is that people with discrete social phobia will show more heart symptoms (like rapid pulse), which is important to know when treating people who suffer from both a heart condition and discrete social phobia, as clearly both of these conditions must be treated.

OBSESSIVE-COMPULSIVE DISORDER

Obsessive-compulsive disorder (OCD) is frequently discussed, joked about, and written about, and many people believe they suffer from it or at least know someone who does. Persons with OCD typically experience persistent, upsetting thoughts that are troubling for them and rituals that they use to control their anxiety, but conversely, it is the rituals and thoughts that end up controlling a significant part of a person's life. Obsessions are uncontrollable, unwanted thoughts that make a person uncomfortable and force them to do something to keep the thoughts and anxiety at bay. Remember the role of control in anxiety disorders in general? Obsession is another example of how the control issue is fundamental to the disorder. People cannot control their thoughts and anxiety (obsessive part), so they engage in rituals that give them a sense of managing (controlling) these thoughts and feelings (compulsive part). Compulsions may include rituals such as checking, counting, performing specific tasks in a specific order, and touching things, but even if these behaviors temporarily relieve the anxiety, it always returns. These rituals are almost like strong superstitions; the person is usually aware that the compulsions are irrational but fears that not performing them would result in something terrible happening, so they do them anyway.

Many people have obsessions or even exhibit compulsive behavior patterns, but that does not mean they have OCD. To qualify for an OCD diagnosis, behavioral patterns have to occur over a long period of time (e.g., months or years) and intrude into a person's life—a person with OCD may have good or bad days, but their symptoms are always present. Obsessions and compulsions can also accompany other psychological disorders, for example, obsessive-compulsive personality disorder (OCPD). A person with this disorder has learned to live with obsessions and compulsions as habits more than symptoms. They are not as intrusive as the same symptoms of OCD, and OCPD lacks an anxiety component. These people experience obsessions without anxiety and become annoyed, perhaps, but not anxious, if prevented from fulfilling their compulsions. Obsessions and/or compulsions are found in other anxiety disorders as well, such as PD or GAD, but they are not as deeply ingrained nor as intrusive as in OCD.

Most adults with OCD know their ideas and behaviors are senseless; they say they feel "crazy" and try to hide their behaviors from others, often very creatively. However, some adult patients and most children with OCD feel that their behavior is perfectly reasonable and understandable, and these patients are diagnosed as having "OCD with poor insight." It is estimated that OCD affects about 2.2 million American adults, many of whom live with other psychological and medical conditions that further complicate their problems. Patients with OCD frequently suffer from eating disorders, other anxiety disorders, or depression, and some self-medicate with alcohol or drugs. Men and women usually have similar rates of OCD (unlike most other anxiety disorders), and it usually emerges in childhood, adolescence, or young adulthood. Some evidence points to a genetic link in this disorder, but even if this is true, genetics alone is not enough to explain the full range of OCD symptoms. OCD can be relatively mild or quite severe, and effective treatments usually include both medication and psychotherapy; one without the other is not as likely to be successful.

The diagnostic criteria used by the *Diagnostic and Statistical Manual* include:

1. Obsessions and/or compulsions
   a. Obsessions involve:
      i. Frequent and uncontrollable thoughts, impulses, or images that seem to intrude on normal life patterns and seem inappropriate in the circumstances; they also cause significant anxiety or distress to the person experiencing them.
      ii. The obsessions are not the same thing as significant worrying about normal concerns.
      iii. Patients will try to control these obsessions with other patterns of acting or thinking in an attempt to "replace" the unwanted thoughts or feelings.
      iv. The patient recognizes that the unwanted thoughts or obsessions come from their own mind and are not put there by an external person or agency.

    b.   Compulsions are:
        i.   Continually repeated acts or thoughts that are intended to reduce or prevent the discomfort produced by the obsessions or to prevent some feared outcome that they think will occur if they do not complete the compulsive act; however, these compulsive behaviors are realistically unrelated to the "cause" of the obsessions or are far excessive to what they are trying to prevent.

2. Most patients will realize that their behavior and fears are unrealistic and excessive, although this does not always apply to children.
3. Obsessions or compulsions will cause significant distress, take an unreasonable amount of time, and will interfere with a person's normal life.
4. The obsessions or compulsions are not a major part of another psychological disorder.
5. The disorder is not due to another medical condition or the influence of a substance of abuse.
6. When making this diagnosis the person who makes it must specify if the patient has good or poor insight into their condition.

OCD exists in all cultures and has been described in a variety of ways throughout history. It also appears that the basic types of obsessions and compulsions are consistent across cultures—that is, people in different countries still tend to have the same types of obsessions and compulsions. The most common types of obsessions are:

1. Fear of contamination (dirt and germs)
2. Pathological doubt
3. Need for symmetry
4. Aggressive obsessions
5. Other obsessions
    a.   Sexual
    b.   Hoarding or collecting
    c.   Religious
    d.   Need to know something or remember things
    e.   Fear of saying certain things
    f.   Fear of not saying the right thing
    g.   Intrusive (but neutral) images
    h.   Intrusive nonsense sounds, words, or music
    i.   Somatic

The most common compulsions are:

1. Checking
2. Washing
3. Symmetry (things have to be "even" or balanced out)
4. Need to ask questions or confess to something
5. Counting
6. Other compulsions
   a. Repeating rituals (doing things over and over again)
   b. Ordering or arranging
   c. Mental rituals other than counting or checking
   d. Touching certain things
   e. Measures to prevent causing harm to self, others, or things

Among children most symptoms are similar to those in adults, although washing compulsions followed by repeating rituals are the most common in children. Most people with OCD have multiple obsessions and compulsions over time with a particular fear or concern dominating at any given time. Some patients will have obsessions without compulsions or vice versa, but this is unusual—they almost always are present together.

OCD may occur with other disorders, and especially with depression, which may pre-date the OCD or be caused by the complications of dealing with OCD. In addition, OCD as well as other disorders can worsen during depression. For example, one patient who had pre-existing OCD was able to work and lead a normal life. However, he suffered a traumatic event at work and developed PTSD. Without question, the PTSD significantly impacted the OCD, worsening the OCD symptoms.

Many believe that there is frequent comorbidity with OCD and Tourette's Syndrome (a type of tic disorder where people say or do things impulsively that they cannot control) or other tic disorders, but the relationship between OCD and these types of disorders is not clear. In patients with Tourette's or tics, there is a greater probability of developing childhood-onset OCD and also more severe OCD symptoms. Another disorder that is sometimes comorbid with OCD is schizophrenia; patients who suffer from schizophrenia or schizoaffective disorder have rates of OCD ranging from 8 to 46 percent depending on the study that you read.

Until the mid-1980s, OCD was considered a rare disorder, but it was found to be the fourth most common mental disorder with a lifetime prevalence rate of 2.5 percent. The reported age of onset is usually during late adolescence. However, people who suffer from OCD will often report that they remember having problems in their childhood, although they covered them up and/or were dismissed and ignored by others. The earlier age of onset has been associated with an increased rate of OCD in immediate family members, suggesting that there is a familial type of OCD characterized by early onset, which usually means that it is more likely to get worse and be more serious.

In terms of differential diagnosis with OCD, there are a number of considerations. First, as mentioned above, obsessions and compulsions can occur within many other disorders besides OCD. To qualify for a diagnosis of OCD, the obsessions cannot be limited to the focus of another disorder like when people are obsessed with their appearance or weight. However, if obsessions or compulsions are preoccupying as well as distressing or impairing, then it is probably OCD. As with other anxiety disorders, OCD uses avoidance to manage anxiety, but it also includes compulsions, which are not common to other anxiety disorders. As many as 60 percent of people with OCD also experience panic attacks, but unlike PD, these attacks only occur with exposure to a feared object or situation (e.g., dirt or contamination). Some severe mental illnesses have obsessive features but rarely have the compulsive component, and in schizophrenia there may be obsessions or compulsions, but there are other symptoms like hallucinations and thought disorders as well. OCD is not a delusional disorder (a disorder characterized by unusual and bizarre beliefs), but some types of delusions (e.g., physical problems, jealousy) may be difficult to differentiate from OCD. However, these disorders will not usually have the anxiety component to the same extent.

Some people confuse impulse control disorders with OCD, since people obsess over what they want to do and may seem compulsive about their inability to control the behavior; but they are not the same thing and will not show the other features of OCD. Therefore, if someone has kleptomania, trichotillomania (obsessive pulling of the hair), pathological gambling, sexual compulsions, etc., this is *not* the same thing as OCD. With impulse control disorders people enjoy or at least want to perform the act in question, while OCD compulsions are not gratifying, although they may temporarily decrease anxiety. Fear and anxiety drive the compulsions in OCD, but this is not true in impulse control disorders.

Causal factors are complex and sometimes confusing in OCD. There are some studies that find abnormalities in the structure of the brains of OCD patients and also problems with how the brain functions. Other neurobiological studies suggest that there is a problem with one of the systems in the brain that deals with the neurotransmitter (chemical messenger) called serotonin, and the medications that are used to treat OCD work with the serotonin system in the brain. Although the evidence of a role for the serotonin system in OCD is compelling, the actual role of serotonin in this disorder is not entirely clear. In some forms of OCD, especially if it occurs with Tourette's, the balance of serotonin and other neurotransmitter systems may be important, and in that case, other kinds of medications may be helpful as well.

There is support for a genetic aspect of OCD, and in monozygotic twins a 63 percent concordance rate (when both twins have the same disorder) is very compelling evidence. However, since the concordance is not 100 percent, there must be environmental factors at work as well. Some studies have found that in families with an OCD patient there are others who may have OCD or other related conditions, and this rate is higher than would be found in the normal population. Other interesting studies have shown that if a person has OCD it is more likely that someone in the family will have Tourette's Syndrome, and if a person in a family has Tourette's it is likely that others in the family may have OCD. Although there is ample evidence pointing to a role for genetics in OCD, it is unlikely that this disorder is a simple genetic disease; clearly, there is a role for the environment in the cause of OCD as well.

A variety of psychological factors have been proposed for the understanding and treatment of OCD, but in recent years most of the attention has focused on learning approaches, with the cognitive and behavioral perspectives predominating. It has been demonstrated that people can acquire OCD even without a genetic component, which suggests that the condition can be acquired by direct learning or observational learning. Also, similar to phobias, it seems that the compulsions in OCD can be strengthened by learning, making it harder to get rid of them. For example, if a person becomes upset and anxious because of an obsession, and then they perform one of their compulsions, if the anxiety decreases even a little bit this means that the person will be more likely to repeat the compulsion in the future when they are obsessing or feeling anxious. Thus, the compulsion is "reinforced" or learned more completely by the reduction in anxiety. Of course, the problem is that this compulsion does not make the anxiety or obsessions go away permanently and, therefore, the condition becomes more deeply entrenched and more difficult to treat and eliminate. Recent theories have integrated some of the psychological and biological/genetic factors in OCD and are trying to create more complex and complete models to understand how OCD is developed as well as improved models of treatment.

A number of effective treatment options involving medication and behavioral types of treatment exist for all age groups with OCD. Children and older adults seem to do very well with behavioral treatments and

tolerate most of the medications we use to treat OCD, although in somewhat lower doses than in adults. The goals of treatment for OCD patients
are to reduce the frequency and intensity of symptoms as much as possible
and to reduce or eliminate the amount of interference the symptoms have
in the person's life. Typically, most patients do not completely rid themselves of OCD but can expect significant improvement with appropriate
treatment. For most people with OCD the condition fluctuates in severity
over time but does not completely go away. One of the reasons why people
may avoid treatment is that, when it seems to be improving, they feel it
may be disappearing and that they do not need to continue treatment.
However, OCD usually reappears and may even get worse. The sooner
patients with OCD seek treatment, the greater the chances that the treatment will be successful.

6

❖

Types of Anxiety Disorders III: Posttraumatic Stress Disorder and Acute Stress Disorder

POSTTRAUMATIC STRESS DISORDER

Numerous historical accounts of the damaging and lasting effects of severe trauma reveal the similarities between humans suffering extreme stress in the distant past and the present. Although the diagnosis of post-traumatic stress disorder (PTSD) is fairly recent, the experiences to which it refers are well known, but often by different names. Not surprisingly, many of the earlier references to what is now called PTSD refer to war-time and battlefield trauma. Some, however, believe that PTSD is not truly a psychological condition but rather an exaggeration used to prove, for political reasons, that warfare is harmful to mental health. However, anyone who is a veteran or a survivor of any type of trauma, or has worked with them, is very aware of the seriousness of this problem. Posttraumatic stress disorder is a very real disorder with very real casualties. People who dismiss PTSD or minimize it are either poorly informed or have their own political agenda, or both.

In recent decades mental health professionals have recognized that some military personnel have experienced events so traumatic that the person is severely and often permanently affected. During the Civil War this condition was known as "battle fatigue," which implied a temporary condition based upon the cumulative effects of being in combat. In World War I it was called "shell shock," a term that evolved due to the increased use of artillery and to soldiers hiding in trenches, hoping that shells would not fall on them and kill them. During World War II doctors began to notice the serious nature of soldiers' reactions to being in combat by labeling it "combat neurosis" or "traumatic neurosis." Even with an increased level of understanding, it was still assumed that people who suffered from this condition were emotionally and psychologically weak or inadequate.

During the Korean War era the DSM I (*Diagnostic and Statistical Manual I*) was created to coordinate and standardize efforts to diagnose mental illnesses. Within the DSM the trauma-induced condition (now referred to as PTSD) was initially called a "gross stress reaction." This was the first war in America's history during which psychological factors received serious attention. However, it was during the Vietnam conflict that an increased awareness of PTSD developed and that the specific term "PTSD" was introduced to the public for this disorder.

Although the earliest focus on PTSD was concerned with the military, much of recent research has been conducted on victims of crime, including sexual assault and rape, as well as victims of natural disasters and catastrophic events such as the 2001 collapse of the World Trade Center towers that occurred as a result of terrorist attacks. In general, three types of symptoms are seen with PTSD:

1. Hyperarousal
   a. Irritability
   b. Increased startle reaction (more "jumpy")
   c. Hypervigilance (notice "every little thing" and feel it is a threat)
   d. Sleep difficulties
   e. Concentration problems
2. Re-experiencing or intrusion
   a. Vivid memories
   b. Nightmares
   c. Re-experiencing the event
   d. Anything that reminds them of the trauma is troubling
3. Avoidance and emotional numbing
   a. Avoidance of feelings, thoughts, persons, places, or situations that evoke the troubling memories
   b. Loss of interest in usual activities

   c. Feeling separated from others and even from their own feelings

   d. Think about the trauma much of the time

PTSD is now routinely recognized in places where natural disasters, war, and catastrophic events occur. Community-based studies find a lifetime prevalence rate of 8 percent for PTSD in the adult population, and, like many other anxiety conditions, women are twice as likely to be diagnosed with PTSD. This suggests that women are exposed to more traumatic events than men. The highest rates of PTSD are found among rape survivors, military combat veterans and prisoners of war, graves registration personnel (people responsible for retrieving dead bodies after a battle), and victims of ethnically and politically motivated imprisonment and genocide. PTSD is often a chronic condition with a significant number of people remaining symptomatic several years following the initial traumatic event and rarely making a full recovery. In fact, at least one-third of those diagnosed with PTSD fail to recover even after many years. However, it is clear that treatment will help to reduce the severity of the symptoms of PTSD and will often shorten the time to remission (when there are no longer any symptoms).

According to the DSM the diagnostic criteria for PTSD include:

1. The person has experienced a traumatic event that includes two things:
   a. The person either experienced, saw, or was involved with something that included the threat of death or serious injury to the person themselves or others; and
   b. The person felt significant fear, helplessness, or horror; in children they may respond with agitation or disorganized behavior.

2. The traumatic event is re-experienced with:
   a. Distressing thoughts or perceptions that happen often and feel uncontrollable; children may actually act out the trauma in their play activities.
   b. Patients may have nightmares about the trauma; children's nightmares may be more unspecific and vague.
   c. Patients may have flashbacks, obsessive thinking, and continual ruminations while children may actually re-enact the trauma.
   d. The victim of the trauma may be very distressed when confronted with anything that reminds them of the traumatic event.
   e. The victim will also have significant physical symptoms in reaction to the re-experience of the trauma.

3. The patient will typically avoid or have a psychological "numbing,"
    which will involve at least three of the following:
    a. Avoidance of thinking, feeling, or talking about the trauma
    b. Avoidance of other people, places, and activities that remind the
        person of the trauma
    c. Inability to remember specific aspects of the trauma
    d. Decreased interest in participating in normally important activities
    e. Feeling detached or estranged from others
    f. Restriction of the normal range of feelings
    g. A sense that they do not have a "normal" future
4. Symptoms of heightened arousal that were not present before the
    trauma and include at least two of the following:
    a. Problems falling asleep or staying asleep
    b. Being more irritable than normal and may have anger outbursts
    c. Difficulty concentrating
    d. Hypervigilant (always on guard)
    e. Heightened startle response
5. These symptoms must continue for at least one month.
6. The symptoms and problems must cause significant distress and/or
    difficulties in functioning in important areas of a person's normal
    life.
7. The diagnosis must also note if the condition is:
    a. Acute—has existed for less than three months
    b. Chronic—has lasted more than three months
    c. Delayed onset—occurs at least six months following the trauma

One difficulty in diagnosing PTSD is that some people can experience symptoms similar to PTSD without experiencing a traumatic event. One study showed that trauma rarely led to PTSD in children and adolescents, but the rates of other psychiatric disorders nearly doubled following a traumatic event. Obviously, people can be significantly impacted by a trauma but may not develop PTSD, although they are higher risk to develop another different type of psychological disorder.

Many people experience symptoms of dissociation following a trauma (e.g., amnesia, feelings of detachment, feelings that they are not the same person, or that things around them seem strange or different). However, since these symptoms are not found universally in PTSD patients, it is questionable if they should be considered as part of that diagnosis. Controversy also persists about the existence of "partial PTSD," when a person has most but not all of the criteria to qualify for the diagnosis. It does seem to be true that these individuals (with "partial PTSD") are also in need of treatment just as someone who presents all of the necessary criteria.

In recent years, discussions about how to define which events are to be considered traumatic have been challenging since what is traumatic to one person may not be to another. PTSD is defined by the apparent cause (trauma) but also by the symptoms exhibited by the person who experiences the trauma. To qualify for the diagnosis of PTSD the person must have experienced an event that meets the criteria that are defined as a trauma in the DSM. Although the lists of specific criteria appear all inclusive, there is still room for a professional's judgment. Community-based studies have shown that over two-thirds of the population will experience at least one traumatic event during the course of their life, and that the more intense the trauma, the more likely it is that the victim will develop PTSD. While this makes sense, we also know that an individual's mental and emotional responses to the trauma are also significant in determining the risk of PTSD, as well as their personality or past experiences. Even some people who are presented with a serious medical diagnosis have demonstrated the necessary criteria for PTSD, and for others the witnessing of medical events can also be traumatic.

Defining "traumatic" is fraught with challenges because of the variability in responses on the part of each person. Recently, we have seen a shift away from focusing on the traumatic event to more consideration for the response of the person. We continue to redefine the term "traumatic event," and it is now apparent that many more people have been exposed to trauma than originally believed. I was asked to be an expert witness in a trial that involved a person claiming to have developed PTSD as a result of a workplace accident. While performing his job this person came in contact with a chemical that he thought to be toxic and deadly; he was significantly traumatized and believed that he was going to die. No one could identify the chemical or the treatment required, and it was quite some time before it was determined that the chemical was not immediately dangerous and did not pose a threat to the health, well-being, and life of the employee. The defense claimed that the chemical was not deadly and, therefore, exposure to the chemical was not a significant traumatic event. My testimony stressed that the experienced trauma was based on the perception of the employee at the time of the event and that PTSD symptoms were present more than a month later. The subsequent discovery that the chemical was not fatal was obviously a relief, but it was not a cure for the already existing disorder. The court agreed and the claim for damages was recognized.

Determining the extent of trauma within a population depends upon the criteria used to define it. Using a broad definition of trauma, more than 60 percent of men and 50 percent of women have experienced at least one trauma in their lives. Clearly, the vast majority of people who experience trauma do not go on to develop PTSD, and one large study found that 90 percent of women and 97 percent of men who experience trauma do not develop PTSD. More than two-thirds of children have experienced a traumatic event and one-third have experienced more than one—often by hearing of or seeing something happen to someone else. However, a small minority of children exposed to trauma present any significant symptoms related to the trauma, and it is uncommon for children to be diagnosed with PTSD.

Generally, women are two to three times more likely to develop PTSD than men due to the different types of trauma they are exposed to. Men tend to experience traumas that involve nonsexual physical violence, and women experience trauma that more often involves rape and childhood sexual abuse, which often occurs over a longer period of time and can have a more profound, long-lasting effect. Of men and women who experience the same event, women are more likely to develop PTSD, although it has not been easy to determine why this occurs. A recent study that some of my coworkers and I conducted reports that, among career professional firefighters, the longer a person has been on the job, the greater the probability they have experienced PTSD or at least developed some symptoms of PTSD. The study also determined that firefighters rarely seek professional help and tend to rely more on humor, emotional support, avoidance, and alcohol use to manage their symptoms. Therefore, there are several questions left to answer: "Are men less likely to develop PTSD or are they less likely to report it and seek help or, perhaps, both?" It is also possible that women are better at soothing and supporting men after a traumatic event than men are at comforting women. Our study also implies that without treatment, the effects of PTSD worsen over time for some people. This is consistent with findings reported on Gulf War veterans that showed an increase in symptoms of PTSD over time, with 3 percent showing signs of PTSD immediately following the war and over 8 percent showing significant symptoms two years later.

Additional factors can affect one's vulnerability for developing PTSD. For example, PTSD is more likely to affect someone who has experienced prior traumatic events or injury (e.g., physical or sexual assault), especially if the victim feels at fault for the trauma; this can increase one's vulnerability for developing PTSD (more so than someone who has experienced natural disasters). Some studies have shown that having a high IQ may blunt the effects of a traumatic event, but having a low IQ tends to increase the intensity of the response. Increased vulnerability to PTSD is also caused by depression, anxiety, alcohol and drug abuse, child-hood behavior disorders, adolescent delinquency, and antisocial personality disorder and other personality disorders. One study found that firefighters who had less confidence in their own abilities and were more hostile were more likely to develop PTSD, and twin and adoption studies suggest there is a genetic factor in determining one's susceptibility to PTSD. Research evidence reveals that some people are concerned about patients "faking" PTSD symptoms in order to obtain disability benefits, but, while this is a valid concern, it is not likely to include a large number of people. In fact, the bigger problem is the large number of valid claims for PTSD disability that are denied when they should be approved. While it seems true that many more people are exposed to trauma than was originally thought, it is becoming increasingly obvious that we need to start paying more attention to the personality and vulnerabilities of the patients who are exposed to trauma rather than trying to find even better ways of describing and defining trauma. As was said above—what is traumatic to one person may not be traumatic to another.

There is evidence that what occurs following the traumatic event may be as important as what happens before—at least in terms of developing PTSD. The range of responses, support, vulnerability factors, and individual personalities all must be considered. It is not surprising that PTSD is frequently misdiagnosed due to its complexities. Some of the reasons it is often misdiagnosed are:

- High rate of comorbidity (having other medical or psychological problems)
- Patient denial or not telling the truth
- Overly high standards for diagnosing PTSD by some practitioners
- Failure to take a trauma history

Complicating both the diagnosis and treatment of PTSD are the high rates of comorbidity that are unfortunately all too common. Studies reveal a lifetime comorbidity rate of PTSD with at least one psychiatric disorder is 88 percent in men and 79 percent in women. The most common comorbid conditions are:

- Mood disorders (50 percent for major depression, 20 percent for dysthymia)

- Other anxiety disorders (16 percent generalized anxiety disorder, 9 percent panic disorder, 30 percent specific phobia, 28 percent social phobia, 19 percent agoraphobia)
- Substance use disorders (52 percent alcohol abuse in men, 34 percent drug abuse in men, 28 percent alcohol abuse in women, 27 percent drug abuse in women)
- Conduct disorder (43 percent in men, 15 percent in women)

The course of PTSD depends upon many factors. Immediately following a trauma, a high percentage of victims will develop a myriad of symptoms, which can include disorganized behavior, dissociative symptoms, behavioral changes, as well as occasional paranoid symptoms (e.g., suspiciousness). The range of resulting outcomes for patients experiencing PTSD includes:

- Full recovery
- Relatively unchanging course with only mild fluctuations
- More obvious fluctuations with intermittent periods of well-being and recurrences of major symptoms
- Deterioration with age in a limited number of cases due to the passage of time with no resolution of symptoms
- Increased startle response, nightmares, irritability, and depression

General medical conditions (e.g., head injury, burns, etc.) can also occur as a direct consequence of trauma. PTSD may be associated with the increased rate of adverse medical conditions such as problems with bones, joints, and muscles, and heart and circulatory difficulties, further complicating the diagnosis, treatment, and outcome of the disorder. The course and outlook of PTSD is often uncertain; in one study less than 28 percent of people who had witnessed a mass killing spree recovered within a year, and, yet, in another study of the same event, 46 percent of patients had developed chronic PTSD. We are now aware that PTSD can last a lifetime due to observed and studied physical changes that occur in the brain following serious trauma. This reason alone makes it vitally important to follow patients with this disorder and ensure that treatment is available whenever it is needed.

ACUTE STRESS DISORDER

Acute stress disorder (ASD) is a condition related to PTSD but is often overlooked. It usually emerges within two days to four weeks following a trauma, and most people who develop PTSD will have already developed ASD. The best description of ASD is: a clinical reaction that occurs after experiencing a trauma and during the time prior to a patient developing and being diagnosed with PTSD. Depending upon which study is reviewed, anywhere from 50 to 80 percent of people with ASD will go on to develop PTSD. Although some wonder if ASD is a milder form of PTSD and should be included with PTSD, the consensus is that ASD is not a minor variant of PTSD since there are significant diagnostic and treatment differences.

According to the DSM the diagnostic criteria for ASD include:

1. Exposure to a trauma during which
   a. there was threatened death or serious injury, or a threat to physical integrity of self or others, and
   b. a response that involves intense fear, helplessness, or horror
2. Experiencing at least three of the following during or following trauma:
   a. Sense of numbing, detachment, or absence of emotional responsiveness
   b. A reduction in awareness of his/her surroundings
   c. Derealization (things do not seem real)
   d. Depersonalization (person feels different than usual)
   e. Dissociative amnesia
3. Re-experiencing the traumatic event in at least one of the following: recurrent images, thoughts, dreams, illusions, flashbacks, or a sense of reliving the experience; or distress on exposure to reminders of the trauma
4. Marked avoidance of stimuli that arouse recollections of the trauma
5. Marked symptoms of anxiety or increased arousal
6. Significant clinical distress or impairment in an important aspect of the person's life.
7. Disturbance lasts at least two days and a maximum of four weeks, and occurs within four weeks of the trauma
8. Reaction is not attributed to the effects of a substance or general medical condition, or is not a brief psychotic episode or an complication of another psychological disorder

Some people question the validity of adding dissociative symptoms to the diagnostic criteria for ASD because there are multiple pathways to PTSD; that is, there are many different ways in which people can contract PTSD, although most of the people with ASD who do not have dissociative symptoms will go on to develop PTSD. One does not have to experience dissociative symptoms to be diagnosed with either ASD or PTSD, although most clinicians feel that dissociative symptoms should remain part of the diagnostic criteria since most people with dissociative disorders have experienced some type of trauma. If symptoms last longer than four weeks, this means the person is suffering from an illness other than ASD. It may be PTSD, but it could be something else depending upon the symptoms present. Not much is known at present about ASD since people don't seek treatment unless their symptoms worsen. However, following an event like rape and assault, acute ASD is found in 70–90 percent of victims. The number who experience dissociative symptoms is not known at this time, although one study showed that those who had been exposed to a firestorm reported a very high incidence of dissociative symptoms.

Although we do not have a clear picture of who is likely to develop ASD, we find similarities with those who develop PTSD. People who experience more severe trauma or have pre-existing psychological problems, have family and genetic vulnerability, have an abnormal personality, lack social support, and experience physical injury are more likely to develop ASD. It is important when diagnosing ASD to determine if any of the symptoms existed prior to the trauma, since this might indicate that a condition that they suffered before the event has worsened due to the traumatic event rather than a new condition developing such as ASD or PTSD. If the ASD symptoms are the result of a physical injury, then the physical condition is probably the most appropriate diagnosis rather than ASD.

The course of ASD has not been well established, although we know that the dissociative and cognitive symptoms that are common in ASD patients improve spontaneously over time in most cases. Reports state that the development of PTSD is more common among ASD patients with dissociative symptoms than those with simple anxiety symptoms; although, as mentioned above, some still question the inclusion of dissociative symptoms in the diagnostic criteria for ASD.

Patients with ASD will often improve with the passing of time or minimal treatment or support. Although most victims of trauma do not develop PTSD and will return to normal functioning within a period of time, those who do develop PTSD will require a higher level of treatment. The high levels of comorbidity and symptom similarity between PTSD and depression and anxiety disorders suggest that the same predisposing factors for these disorders are probably operative in PTSD patients as well. This means that anyone who is high risk for anxiety or depression is also higher risk for ASD and PTSD following a trauma. There is evidence of some physical differences in the bodies of people suffering from PTSD including their brain structures and how their brains function. However, many findings are not clear if these were pre-existing conditions that might have been vulnerability factors or if they were the result of changes in the body in response to significant trauma and stress.

SOME CAUSAL FACTORS AND TREATMENTS FOR PTSD

Additional factors may affect the development of PTSD, such as simple conditioning or learning, which can explain why certain stimuli become related to the experience of trauma and then lead to similar feelings later. This relationship can also be important for treatment options. Some practitioners have found that behavioral treatments using exposure to stimuli associated with fear or discomfort following the trauma could be helpful in treating PTSD. Scant but consistent evidence also shows that social support can be helpful to those suffering from PTSD, especially when the trauma involves the loss of a significant source of support. It appears that social support is a buffer that helps to minimize the effects of trauma, but the lack of social support places someone at additional risk for PTSD. Another risk factor for PTSD is the presence of anxiety or depressive disorders among family members. Evidence suggests that the psychiatric history of the person or of family members can influence two risk factors: first, it increases the likelihood of being exposed to a trauma; and second, it increases the risk of developing PTSD once the person experiences trauma.

A person who is exposed to trauma is at higher risk for several psychiatric illnesses including depression, some anxiety disorders, and PTSD, and treatment depends primarily on the types of symptoms presented and in what order. In addition to medical treatments (specific medication for specific symptoms), a number of psychological approaches are offered, including cognitive-behavioral therapy (CBT) and exposure therapy, anxiety management training, and cognitive therapy. Here are some guidelines for the administration of treatment following a trauma:

- Brevity (keep it short and to the point)
- Immediacy (administer treatment soon after the trauma, if possible)
- Centrality (deal with issues central to the trauma)
- Expectancy (meet and explore the person's expectations for treatment)
- Proximity (treat the person close to the site of trauma, if possible)
- Simplicity (keep the treatment simple, straightforward)

Civilian trauma survivors who developed ASD resorted to cognitive strategies of self-punishment and worry more than survivors without ASD. Treating survivors with CBT has reduced these strategies and has increased the use of reappraisal and social control strategies. Those who are highest risk for traumatic stress disorders and who should be identified for treatment first include:

- Survivors with a psychiatric disorder
- Traumatically bereaved people
- Children, especially when separated from parents
- Individuals who are particularly dependent on psychosocial supports:
  ○ elderly
  ○ handicapped
  ○ mentally retarded
- Traumatized survivors
- Body handlers

Although evidence shows that some people are more likely to benefit from treatment following trauma, there is still no evidence to suggest that all survivors of trauma should be treated—screened, perhaps, but not necessarily treated. In fact, critical incident stress debriefing group sessions did not reduce the risk of developing PTSD later, and sometimes it seemed to worsen the symptoms. It appears that the best strategy is to first allow people to settle into their own coping styles and then offer treatment to those who do not improve.

One type of individual who should be typically targeted for treatment following trauma is a person with a history of aggression, since PTSD is one path to increasing aggressiveness. In returning war veterans, there have been concerns regarding the increased possibility of intimate partner violence once back at home. To determine who is at higher risk for domestic or intimate partner violence, it is important to determine how much and what is perceived by them as a threat in the domestic environment. Although treatments that are used for typical PTSD patients are also helpful in dealing with violent tendencies in these patients, some interesting research has involved conjoint treatment for PTSD patients and their partners. This type of treatment involves:

- Psychoeducation to help the patient and their partner understand how PTSD affects their relationship
- Training in behavioral skills that improves listening and paraphrasing, assertiveness, and communication; the couple is taught to express emotions and to externalize and analyze their thoughts

- Taking newly learned skills and using them to improve communication and their relationship and to develop more trust and security

SUMMARY

Trauma will always be a factor that will cause problems in people's lives, and sometimes these problems will become significant disruptions. One of the things that makes many events traumatic is that they may be unforeseeable, unanticipated, and nothing that could be avoided by the person in question. Consequently, it is typically not the sort of thing that people could have prevented by careful planning or just being "smarter." However, such things as walking alone in a strange neighborhood late at night, drinking and driving, or "having fun" with high-risk behaviors can and do lead to traumatic events, but when these types of things happen the victim probably does not anticipate the traumatic outcome, and even if they do, research shows that when people blame themselves for a trauma it is even a bigger problem for them and harder to treat.

Suffice it to say that trauma will always be a part of the human condition in one way or another, and learning how to avoid it when possible is best, but often this is not possible. Therefore, we need to do a better job of dealing with victims of trauma sooner and more effectively. Having timely and appropriate treatment for victims of trauma may not eliminate either trauma or all of the psychological results of it, but good and responsive treatment will reduce the impact of trauma on people's lives and hopefully keep the results of trauma from scarring the victim for life.

7

❖

Treatments for
Anxiety Disorders

Treatments for anxiety disorders offer varying degrees of success depending upon the accuracy and timeliness of the diagnosis, the type of treatment, the experience of the mental health professional, and the patient's personal commitment to treatment. However, those who are in need of treatment often do not receive it due to a lack of awareness of available treatment options and/or poor access to treatment opportunities. Since anxiety disorders are often initially identified at the primary care level, it is encouraging to note that in recent years physicians are more aware of anxiety disorders and the basic types of treatments that are available. When primary care providers and other professionals (especially mental health providers) communicate with one another and coordinate the care of the patient, treatment is usually successful.

The primary goals of treatment involve reducing troublesome symptoms as well as helping the patient cope with situations more effectively that may be linked to their anxiety symptoms. Health care providers must also focus on decreasing the feelings of emotional numbness that can accompany anxiety disorders and on helping patients to stay actively involved in normal activities and to resist the temptation to withdraw and avoid others.

Additional treatment goals can help a patient learn to interpret events more realistically instead of exaggerating the risks they fear from ordinary and nonthreatening situations. Learning new and more appropriate responses and helping patients to improve their social functioning, as well as their ability to relax and engage in leisure activities, helps a person feel more competent and in control and fosters feelings of improved self-esteem, trust, and safety. Further, helping people to develop, utilize, and trust their support systems is also an important part of a comprehensive treatment plan, and, occasionally, there is a need to address important issues from a person's past.

Finally, being aware of a patient's additional psychological and medical conditions is important in developing a comprehensive treatment plan. Often, patients enter treatment with multiple anxiety diagnoses, mood disorders, personality disorders, or other problems. One common challenge in treating anxiety disorders involves dealing with the abuse of alcohol or other drugs. While these substances can temporarily lessen anxiety, alcohol and drugs often lead to addictions and serious complications that can make treatment and recovery even more difficult.

In general, anxiety disorders are treated with medication, psychotherapy, or both, depending on the patient's preferences and the approaches of the treating professionals. Some patients will begin treatment without mentioning to their therapist that they have tried and discontinued treatment in the past and are embarrassed for having "failed" the earlier efforts. It is important for those with anxiety disorders to understand that the "failures" are most often due to patients dropping out of treatment too early because they mistakenly believe that treatment is not working or, conversely, that they are cured. Many times the patient has simply not stayed with treatment long enough for it to be effective, but it is important for the new treating professional to be aware of previous treatments and their results.

Medication is often the first type of treatment offered because it produces the quickest results and is usually the only type of treatment available at the primary care level. This can be either a positive or a negative step. While medication helps to reduce the symptoms of anxiety, it is rarely an adequate treatment by itself. However, when symptoms are under better control, the patient can pursue psychotherapeutic types of treatment that are more likely to produce effective and lasting results.

In addition to medication, psychotherapy has been successful in treating anxiety disorders, and there is considerable professional literature supporting its successes. The most recommended and thoroughly evaluated therapy is cognitive-behavioral therapy (CBT), which together with medication is most effective in treating anxiety disorders and in helping to reduce disability from anxiety disorders, thus improving the quality of patients' lives.

Treatment for anxiety disorders does not always require medication, and some patients and providers prefer treatment without psychiatric drugs. There are many forms of psychotherapy and relaxation methods that can be helpful in reducing the symptoms of various anxiety disorders. Other patients will use yoga, meditation, and self-hypnosis. In addition, a comprehensive treatment plan must include adequate sleep, vigorous exercise, appropriate social activities, and proper nutrition, such as healthy eating options and avoiding caffeine and alcohol.

MEDICAL TREATMENTS FOR ANXIETY DISORDERS

Medications are the most common medical treatments for anxiety disorders, with several different successful drug strategies available and with proven effectiveness. While the overall function of drug therapy is to reduce symptoms to manageable levels so that patients can return to a higher level of functioning and an improved quality of life, prescribing the appropriate drug(s) at the correct dosage is often complex and challenging. Sometimes PCPs are reluctant to resort to several drugs at the same time and are more likely to rely upon a relatively limited range of medications. In addition, patients in some communities may only have a limited number of psychiatrists or medically trained mental health professionals who can write prescriptions and often face a lengthy waiting period for an appointment. As the only available professional who can prescribe psychotropic medications, the PCP may delay referring their patients to mental health professionals while they assess the effectiveness of the prescribed medication. This can result in a late referral, the delay of needed behavioral treatment, or lack of any referral at all.

ANTIDEPRESSANT MEDICATIONS

The first line of medical treatment for anxiety disorders is usually the selective serotonin reuptake inhibitors (SSRIs), which are relatively new drugs on the mental health scene. Although they were first used as antidepressants, they are also widely used for anxiety (Prozac is the most well-known of this class of drugs). The SSRIs are frequently used because they are generally well tolerated by most people and the side effects tend to be mild. Interestingly, if a person has side effects to one SSRI this does not necessarily mean that they will have the same side effects with another SSRI.

Another class of drugs called serotonin and norepinephrine reuptake inhibitors (SNRI) tend to produce more side effects but can be helpful if SSRIs are not effective in moderating anxiety. One specific SNRI, Trazadone, produces the side effect of sedation and is often more helpful treating insomnia than anxiety, but it can also be used in combination with other medications when sleep is an issue.

The tricyclic group of antidepressant medications (TCAs) is also used to treat anxiety disorders, although not usually as a first line treatment due to their side effects. TCAs are an older class of drugs that have been in use for decades, but since the introduction of SSRIs they are less frequently prescribed for anxiety or depression. TCAs often have side effects and tend to cause sedation, drying (e.g., mouth, eyes, nose), weight gain, and heart irregularities. Interestingly, these drugs can be used in low doses to treat chronic pain disorders and to prevent migraines, as well as aiding sleep in some patients. Unlike most of the TCAs, Clomipramine (Anafranil) is occasionally used for patients with obsessive-compulsive disorder but is rarely used for other anxiety conditions. Another related medication, a tetracyclic called Mirtazapine (Remeron), is beneficial in treating anxiety and is fairly sedating; it can thus be helpful with insomnia—particularly if taken at bedtime. However, it is rarely used as a first line treatment due to undesirable side effects, including significant weight gain. Of course, not all patients will experience every side effect, but Mirtazapine is not as often used to treat anxiety disorders as there are other medications with fewer troublesome side effects.

The oldest class of antidepressants still used to treat anxiety disorders is the class of drugs called the monoamine oxidase inhibitors (MAOIs). These drugs are rarely used in the United States but are more frequently prescribed in Europe and in other parts of the world. MAOIs have proven to be very effective in treating some types of anxiety disorders, especially panic disorder and social phobia. However, they can cause potentially serious side effects and are dangerous when taken with certain foods and with other medications. Recently, a skin patch for an MAOI was introduced and will probably prove to be much safer, but it has not been available for long and more research is needed.

ANTIANXIETY (ANXIOLYTIC) MEDICATIONS

In addition to the antidepressant medications, another class of drugs that has been used to treat anxiety disorders for many decades is the antianxiety or anxiolytic medications, commonly known as tranquilizers. Tranquilizers are generally quick acting and effective for anxiety—often taking effect within an hour or less. This differs significantly from most of the previously mentioned antidepressants, which may take a month or more to reach full effectiveness. Prior to the introduction of SSRIs, tranquilizers were frequently used to treat anxiety, and at one point, Valium was the most frequently prescribed medication in the United States.

As effective as tranquilizers can be, they are less frequently prescribed today because they are addictive if taken for a long period of time and at a high enough dose. Also, increased tolerance can become an issue, which means a patient needs to continually increase the dosage for it to be effective. They will also cause mild cognitive changes and drowsiness, a concern particularly for the elderly due to the increased risk of falling. People who take tranquilizers should also note that there are 26 percent more motor vehicle accidents when people are taking tranquilizers, and these drugs are very dangerous when used in conjunction with other drugs such as alcohol. Tranquilizers can also be useful for insomnia, as a muscle relaxant for many types of injuries, and for patients who are withdrawing from alcohol. Due to the addictive properties of tranquilizers, it is important for patients who are planning to discontinue a tranquilizer to do so gradually and under the supervision of their physician or prescribing professional.

One additional anxiolytic drug is Buspirone (BuSpar), a safe drug with mild side effects that is nonaddicting and nonsedating. However, as a mild-acting drug it is typically not very effective for moderate to severe anxiety problems. It can be used, however, for mild anxiety. Another class of antianxiety drugs is the beta blockers, primarily used to treat high blood pressure and other cardiovascular issues. However, beta blockers tend to be mildly anxiety reducing and are often helpful with specific social phobias, such as stage fright. Another type of drug that is sometimes used for anxiety is the antihistamine class. This includes allergy medications like Benadryl, but there are also some antihistamines that are used primarily for anxiety (e.g., Hydroxyzine). This is a very safe class of drugs and is not addictive, although they do tend to be mildly sedative and people should be careful when using them as they will increase the risk of things like motor vehicle accidents and falls. They are helpful with mild anxiety but are not usually effective with moderate to severe anxiety.

ADDITIONAL MEDICATIONS AND NATURAL SUBSTANCES

Some people have tried herbs and other "natural" substances as treatments for anxiety disorders with some interesting anecdotal testimonies to their effectiveness. For example, kava has been tried and, although there is no scientific evidence that it works, some attest to its value. Although it is marketed as a "natural" treatment for anxiety, the Federal

Drug Administration (FDA) recently warned that kava may cause liver damage and that long-term use can lead to allergies, visual disturbances, difficulties maintaining balance, and other problems. The FDA also states that kava should not be used during pregnancy or while breast-feeding and should never be used with other antidepressants. Valerian root is another natural substance that is taken primarily for insomnia, and, while it is also marketed for anxiety, there is very little data attesting to its effectiveness. Some have tried St. John's wort for anxiety, although it is primarily used for depression, and the evidence as to its effectiveness in treating anxiety is minimal at best.

Some people feel that taking "natural" substances is better than taking manufactured drugs because they are cheaper and safer—a very misleading perspective. "Natural" does not necessarily mean beneficial or safe! There are many poisonous and dangerous plants growing naturally that can be used as medicine, and we have yet to identify all of their biological effects when they are taken. Use of "natural" substances to treat psychiatric conditions, including anxiety, is possibly dangerous, deadly, or irresponsible at best. First, herbal and alternative substances do not fall under the purview of the FDA, and there is no established scientific body that provides reliable research and credible sources for claims of effectiveness and safety. People who sell these products, of course, claim otherwise, and even if their intentions are good they are placing people at risk. Without coordinated scientific efforts to examine and evaluate effectiveness; side effects; and drug interactions with prescribed and other medications (medical and psychiatric), other natural substances, and foods, to name just a few, it is potentially dangerous for the public to depend upon alternative substances as treatment for a psychiatric condition. If a patient is interested in taking natural substances, I recommend strongly that they seek information and advice from their physician and from a licensed professional trained in the use of alternative treatments. This professional (e.g., psychiatrist, physician's assistant or nurse practitioner, some psychologists, some pharmacists) can advise the patient regarding the risks and potential benefits of the alternative treatment and will have information about side effects, potential drug interactions, and other complications to be aware of.

PSYCHOLOGICAL TREATMENTS OF ANXIETY DISORDERS

As far back as Sigmund Freud in the late 19th and early 20th centuries, professionals have attempted to employ purely psychotherapeutic methods without any medications to treat anxiety disorders. In fact, Charcot, a French psychopathologist (a specialist who studies abnormal psychology), demonstrated that the symptoms of "hysteria" could be temporarily relieved with hypnosis, a clear indication that this disorder could be treated with nonmedical types of therapies. Today, the evidence is clear that medication, while helpful in treating anxiety disorders, is rarely a cure by itself.

The most recommended psychotherapy for anxiety disorders is cognitive-behavioral therapy (CBT), an effective treatment that is used in treating a wide variety of anxiety disorders including obsessive-compulsive disorder. A variety of CBT techniques can be tailored to the individual and their symptoms, as well as to different groups and ages, and in many different settings. Well-controlled studies have consistently shown CBT to significantly reduce anxiety symptoms in children and youths as well as adults and the elderly. This type of therapy is not just a list of techniques used for every patient. More accurately, CBT is an approach that relies upon the use of many different techniques that are designed to deal with each unique situation and individual. It focuses primarily on the changing of particular behaviors, developing better strategies for managing troublesome situations, and learning how to think about, perceive, and interpret circumstances in ways that lead to a healthier adaptation to conditions that are producing the symptoms.

CBT is not usually considered a "quick fix," although some techniques are considered short-term oriented. Research suggests that a patient may not notice significant improvement with CBT for twelve weeks or more, which is why patients who are receiving CBT will also take medication and why patients sometimes terminate their own therapy too soon. Although CBT offers significant treatment results and has proven effective in a variety of settings and over extended follow-up periods, there is still much to learn about the prevention of anxiety disorders and the advantages of early treatment.

CBT involves many factors that must be addressed in order to produce the desired behavioral changes and reach the goals established by the patient and the treating professional. Advocates of CBT believe that chronic negative thinking (cognitive factors) leads to feeling poorly both physically and emotionally (emotional factors), which then leads people to do things (behavioral factors), which tends to perpetuate or intensify the negative thinking and feelings. CBT teaches people how to break this cycle by changing how they act (behavior) and think (cognitive), which will then lead to feeling differently. Research support for CBT is very positive and indicates that patients going through CBT treatment for any type of anxiety disorder usually feel much better following treatment.

Cognitive techniques in CBT attempt to change the way people think about their problems and about the issues that face them. A therapist helps the patient to recognize and view the situations or stimuli that produce anxiety and to develop cognitive strategies for dealing with them in a more functional manner.

In addition to cognitive strategies CBT relies heavily on behavioral techniques, especially during the beginning phases of treatment. It is easier for a patient to change how they act than how they think, and it is easier to change how they think than how they feel. Therefore, treatment begins by working to change the easiest thing first—behavior. By helping people to behave differently in a situation where previously they were too anxious to act normally, they will begin to feel safe enough to try new behaviors. Using exposure methods also helps them to face situations that were previously very frightening, thereby gaining self-confidence and reducing the need to avoid the situation or situations that produce their feelings of anxiety. Patients need to understand that only few hours a month of psychotherapy are not going to change entrenched behavioral patterns, but the patient's efforts outside of the therapy office in their daily life routine will determine how quickly they notice improvements.

The use of exposure techniques in CBT means repeated and systematic confrontation of the feared situations but in a manner that is manageable and safe, stressing that the feared outcome does not actually occur—the anxiety then decreases or disappears. Exposure, or at least exposure-like principles, is the common theme in most of the new treatment methods, and the majority of studies indicate that these techniques are frequently a success. As effective and helpful as CBT appears to be for anxiety disorder, practitioners who are not well-trained or who do not follow the accepted methods produce less impressive results.

There are variants of CBT, as well as several types of therapy that are not CBT, and many of them utilize some of the same techniques. Most schools of therapy for anxiety realize that the use of cognitive techniques must include an element of *exposure* in order to be effective. For example, the treatment of PTSD involves a number of therapies, but the preponderance of modern evidence says that the primary effective component of PTSD treatment is prolonged exposure to troubling or anxiety-provoking stimuli or situations. Many behavioral techniques such as relaxation training, meditation, mindfulness therapy, yoga, and biofeedback frequently help people to manage their anxiety, which helps them to minimize the worry and resultant fears. The chosen approach to treatment often involves a strategy for targeting the most troublesome symptoms first or, in some cases, for dealing with other significant medical or psychological conditions first before tackling the anxiety issues. For example, if a person suffers from an anxiety disorder, as well as a substance use disorder, treating the anxiety while the person is still abusing the substance is counterproductive. It is often difficult to convince a patient of this fact due to their limited understanding of anxiety and their mistaken assumption that, by eliminating their anxiety, they will also eliminate the need to drink or use drugs. However, the process actually works in reverse. The use of a substance negatively affects the anxiety, making the anxiety symptoms more difficult to treat, and the use of drugs or alcohol complicates the effectiveness of the medications prescribed and/or can be a danger in combination.

OTHER PSYCHOSOCIAL TREATMENT APPROACHES

One recent area of study in the cognitive treatment of anxiety disorders focuses on cognitive bias. This refers to the tendency of people with anxiety problems to perceive or think about certain things in a biased or exaggerated fashion—i.e., to magnify the actual risk or probability of a given feared outcome. Although it has been demonstrated that anxious people will selectively attend to and interpret situations in ways that are consistent with their fears, the use of an approach called cognitive bias modification has been very successful in reducing symptoms of anxiety and depression and in adapting to other forms of therapy. Relaxation training is another approach for treating anxiety disorders, and this is also frequently used with other forms of therapy.

Some other creative clinicians have proposed combining a variety of techniques that can take advantage of the fact that many teens seem to be heavily involved with technology. For example, a technology-based form of treatment for anxiety is the application of internet and computer-based CBT (ICT); the intent is to reduce the cost and improve the availability of treatment. As exciting and helpful as this can be, it is also clear that it is not equally effective with all types of anxiety disorders.

Additional forms of treatment include psychodynamic therapies, and many maintain that these methods have been overlooked in the treatment of anxiety disorders and should be considered a mainline treatment. Psychodynamic therapists typically view the interpretation of the traumatic events that are associated with symptoms as being critical to determining the experience and impact of the anxiety disorders. Treatment is then geared in order to alter how patients see the causes of their symptoms by slow exposure and through confrontation and awareness of the negative emotions that have been generated by the real or imagined trauma.

This usually provokes certain troublesome conflicts that must be confronted. The key in this type of treatment is to keep the level of a patient's reactions to confrontations within tolerable limits.

A less frequently utilized treatment technique is hypnosis, which is used to desensitize patients to feared stimuli and situations or as a helpful tool in teaching relaxation techniques. However, a strong warning is offered: hypnosis is not a legally licensed profession, and many who dabble in it are not adequately or professionally trained. Many hypnotists advertise memberships to official-sounding organizations with no legal or professional merit. If a patient wants to try hypnosis to help treat an anxiety disorder, they should find a licensed professional (e.g., psychologist, psychiatrist, or social worker) who is trained specifically in hypnosis. Since the research literature is not supportive of hypnosis as a primary treatment method for anxiety disorders, it is not a widely accepted technique. Some controlled research found that the use of hypnosis is no more effective than doing nothing; however, it might occasionally be helpful in the hands of a competent professional who uses it as a part of a total treatment program. Many people harbor serious misconceptions about the effectiveness of hypnosis and mistakenly think that being hypnotized a couple of times will force their anxiety to disappear—unfortunately, it is never that simple.

Eye movement desensitization and reprogramming (EMDR) therapy has attracted considerable attention in recent years, especially in the treatment of PTSD. This approach relies on a variety of techniques that are supposed to treat the symptoms of anxiety disorders. In addition to PTSD, EMDR has been used to treat phobias, panic disorder, grief, chemical dependency, and dissociative disorders. A major study by the Institute of Medicine did not find that EMDR was an effective treatment for PTSD and that the effects, if any, were not strong. Although there are claims of the successful use of EMDR, most of the confirmatory results were based solely on self-report measures and individual case studies but not on well-controlled research. Physiological measures of the effects of trauma did not support the treatment claims for EMDR. In fact, many studies reported that there was no evidence of therapeutic effect at all.

One new strategy that is gaining considerable attention and support is mindfulness meditation, an acceptance-based approach to dealing with psychological problems. This approach incorporates some cognitive techniques with relaxation types of therapy and looks very promising. What is particularly helpful is that this approach is easily incorporated into other treatment methods, including CBT and most other forms of psychotherapy, and is generating both interest and research. Recent studies demonstrate that mindfulness meditation training can produce a significant reduction in anxiety and depression following treatment, and that the number of patients who reported panic attacks also decreases.

Some providers have focused more on the acceptance aspects of treatment, emphasizing the notion that commitment to treatment on the part of the patient is an important element when dealing with anxiety disorders. The approach is often referred to as acceptance and commitment therapy (ACT), similar to other mindfulness types of treatments. The research literature finds that ACT may be an effective treatment for a variety of disorders, including several anxiety disorders. Although newer mindfulness and ACT approaches are encouraging, more research and experience is necessary to determine how to effectively employ these techniques.

SUMMARY

In examining the various cognitive and behavioral approaches to treatment, it appears that they share more in common than not and that the combination of the different approaches may be helpful to an overall treatment plan. Similarly, many have studied the combination of medication and CBT and feel that it is the best and most comprehensive approach to treating anxiety disorders. However, the literature does not find that the outcome of CBT itself is improved by combining it with medication. While this might seem to argue against the use of medication in the treatment of anxiety disorders, there are enough findings that demonstrate a useful role for medication in treatment for it not to be discounted. Therefore, if a patient is seeking treatment for anxiety problems and wants to avoid medication, there are several effective psychosocial treatments that can be used without medication. A promising approach used more frequently today takes advantage of the short-term benefits of medication, when appropriate, and couples it with the long-term benefits of psychosocial treatments. Many available and effective therapies can be combined to offer an encouraging variety of accepted and successful treatment methods that will help to improve the lives of patients.

8

Living with Anxiety Disorders

WHO NEEDS TREATMENT?

Everyone feels anxious from time to time, but there are two diagnostically relevant factors that set those who need treatment for an anxiety disorder apart from those who do not:

- First, do the symptoms produce significant distress in the person?
- Second, do the symptoms contribute to dysfunction in one or more of the important areas of a person's life (work, relationships, social, school, etc.)?

Suffering from a clinical disorder means that the symptoms are consistent with the diagnostic criteria found in the *Diagnostic and Statistical Manual* and significantly affect daily life—not just cause temporary discomfort or a bad day.

Some people will resist treatment by denying their anxiety difficulties or claiming "they can deal with it," which explains why some people try to reduce their anxiety symptoms through the use of drugs and/or alcohol. This "solution," of course, only makes the symptoms worse and will lead to new and more complex problems. Some symptoms of anxiety are physical in nature (e.g., racing heart, rapid and shallow breathing, difficulty swallowing, etc.) and are responsible for leading many patients to initially consult with their family doctor in hope of finding a physical illness that can be treated and cured. When a person is trying to decide if treatment is needed for an anxiety disorder, they should consider listening to those around them—others often spot problems before the patient recognizes them. The concerns of others might not indicate that a person suffers from an anxiety disorder, but they might suggest some important questions and a reason to seek a professional opinion.

WHERE TO SEEK TREATMENT?

Most people will begin the search for a mental health professional by visiting their primary care physician (PCP), who is familiar with their medical history. Often, the PCP initially will prescribe a medication to calm acute symptoms and may follow it with a referral to a mental health professional if the symptoms do not respond to medication alone. Also, members of the clergy are often trained to provide basic and spiritual counseling and are another source of advice and of referrals to mental health professionals. The school nurse, guidance counselor, school psychologist, or school social workers are additional resources for students and their parents. College students can seek assistance or a referral at either their college's counseling center or their academic or residence advisors; the Dean of Students Office is also a good place to ask where mental health resources are available.

Many companies offer employee assistance programs where an employee can seek confidential short-term counseling or the names of professionals for additional help. The human resources or personnel department at places of employment can be a source of advice and referrals as well. Most medical insurance companies keep a list of participating professionals, usually by zip code, which can be accessed via telephone or web sites. The psychological association of each state or local area is in the telephone book and they can refer a patient to an appropriate psychologist. Further, one can directly call licensed psychologists who are typically listed in the yellow pages.

Psychiatrists are medical doctors (MDs or DOs) and are found under "Physicians" in the telephone book both alphabetically and by specialty, and most county medical societies can make referrals as well. Many counties, hospitals, or communities have outpatient mental health clinics where people can seek psychological or psychiatric assistance, and often they will accept clients who do not have insurance or who may think that they cannot afford treatment. Colleagues, friends, and family may know of a competent professional, but be sure to consult with your PCP first. Victims of a crime can call the Office of Victim Services or the Bureau of Crime Victims in your state or city and ask if they are eligible to receive services, and veterans of the military can call the local Veterans' Administration and ask about available mental health services.

TYPES OF MENTAL HEALTH PROFESSIONALS

How do you choose the appropriate type of mental health professional from the many different titles, professions, and licenses that you might encounter? As a general rule, it is safer to see a professional who is licensed by your state or relevant licensing body. Each state sets its own professional standards and usually has its own professional licensing board; one state may require a therapist to hold a license to practice in a certain profession, but some states do not; insurance companies set their own standards for participating providers, requiring proof of degrees, license, continuing education, and training. One way to gain a better understanding of the covered services and available providers is to call your insurance company. The mental health professions offer a variety of services under the following provider titles:

Psychologist: has a doctoral degree, usually a PhD, PsyD, or EdD, and includes such specialties as clinical, counseling, neuropsychology, industrial/organizational, forensic, school, educational, and many others offering a wide range of nonmedical services.

Psychiatrist: has an MD (doctor of medicine) or a DO (doctor of osteopathy) plus additional training for providing mental health services and is licensed to prescribe medications and conduct other medical treatments.

Nurse Practitioners (NP), Psychiatric Nurse Practitioners (PNP), or Physician's Assistants (PA): usually have a four-year college degree or a nursing degree (or both), have additional training in mental health services, and can write prescriptions and provide other medical services, but only under the supervision (or collaboration) of or with a physician.

Social Worker: has a master's degree in social work, although some have a bachelor's degree in social work and work under supervision in a more limited context. Other social workers may have a doctorate degree, but these usually work in academic settings—although they can treat patients as well. Social workers generally provide individual, group, and family counseling.

MSN: Master's of science in nursing involves nurses who have additional training to provide specific mental health services to patients.

APRN: Advanced practice registered nurse is an RN who has additional training but not at the master's level.

Psychotherapist: is not a regulated or recognized profession; it is simply a title used by many degree holders or licensed professionals who provide psychotherapy services.

Counselor/Therapist: is a title used by many who provide a variety of counseling services including family, marriage, pastoral, guidance, sex, career, school, college, addiction, alcohol, and drug; does not require a specific degree or training, although some states license master's-level providers who offer specific counseling services.

Alcohol/Drug Counselor: requires certification, training, and/or accreditation for these paraprofessionals and can vary from state to state; can include a college degree or just online courses and minimal training and are limited to providing counseling *only* for substance abuse issues unless they hold licenses or certifications in other areas as well.

Clients who are seeking treatment from a licensed professional can be assured that they are receiving care from a provider who has met the standards for education and training and who will be held accountable for meeting ethical and professional standards of care in their profession. In most states, licensed professionals include psychologists, psychiatrists, and social workers. In other states, subdoctoral mental health specialties are licensed to provide some specific services, such as mental health counselors, family counselors, and others. Of course, master's-level providers do not have the depth or breadth of training as doctoral providers, but may be helpful for specific and simpler types of problems.

Since there are misconceptions about the differences between psychologists and psychiatrists, one way to remember this is that a psychiatrist is trained in medicine and then goes on to specialize in the use of medications and other medical treatments for mental illness. A psychologist is a doctoral-level mental health provider with a PhD (doctor of philosophy), a PsyD (doctor of psychology), or an EdD (doctor of education). Licensed psychologists who provide mental health services are usually clinical psychologists or counseling psychologists. The PhD degree means that psychologists, in addition to learning about mental health issues and treatments, are trained in theory and do major research in an original area. The PsyD degree focuses more on clinical practice with some exposure to theory and research, but not as intensely as the PhD. The EdD degree is primarily in education and sometimes includes a counseling degree from a college of education to provide general counseling as well as school-based interventions. They are also usually trained in theory and research, but typically with an educational emphasis. Most psychologists, unlike other mental health specialists, are also trained to administer and interpret psychological tests. In some states and in the Department of Defense, some psychologists receive significant additional training and are able to prescribe medications, but, unlike psychiatrists, they do not get involved with other medical treatments like ECT.

IS TREATMENT WORKING, AND WHEN IS IT COMPLETED?

The effects of treatment are often subtle and results are sometimes slow to emerge. Determining whether treatment is helping can occasionally be difficult, but clearly stating the criteria and goals early in treatment and then following the patient's progress will help track the gains that are being made. During the initial consultation, the provider must complete a full assessment, formulate a diagnostic picture, and begin to develop a treatment plan. The therapist then discusses the findings and treatment options with the client, including medication, psychotherapy, or both. The provider should be prepared to discuss the advantages and disadvantages of various treatment options and encourage input from the patient in order to determine the level of understanding, preferences, and expectations. Goals should be realistic and attainable, as well as the methods of evaluating progress and setting a termination target. For example, challenging a client's statement of "I want to feel better" by asking for specific examples of changes that they would like to see in their daily lives would help to clarify for the provider the patient's understanding and expectations of treatment. Goals such as not having to miss work due to anxiety, keeping anxiety levels low enough to be able to accomplish daily tasks, and being in a more positive mood on most days are specific and yet realistic expectations. As difficult as it is to precisely measure subjective criteria, it is helpful if clients can track their progress in small steps toward attainable goals. Consequently, it is vital that patients attend regularly scheduled appointments and avoid cancelling or missing appointments that create gaps in treatment. In an effort to discourage last-minute cancellations by patients and to be able to provide emergency appointments when needed, most offices require a 24-hour notice to change or cancel an appointment. Just as importantly, providers should inform clients of future dates when they will be unavailable in the office and who will be on call in their place if such arrangements have been made. Most practices now require that patients pay the required copay or coinsurance fee at the time of each visit rather than billing patients later. Not only does this significantly reduce the cost of running an office but it is also an expression of commitment on the part of the patient to the treatment process. Being responsible and remembering the form of payment is often an indication of a patient's personal investment in the treatment.

It is not uncommon for patients and providers to change goals or expectations during treatment as new situations arise, but it is important that they collaboratively discuss the changes and re-establish the new goals, expectations, and criteria. In fact, it is helpful to occasionally revisit these issues during treatment to ensure that the original plan is still appropriate and make modifications if necessary and agreed upon. Sometimes a client or provider will notice that they are not relating well to each other, or the relationship is uncomfortable, which may be due to a client who prefers a therapist of a different gender, age or generation, nationality, or culture, in a different office setting, or with a different style of interacting. Not every therapist will be appropriate for every patient, and it is important that a provider give the patient an opportunity to express their feelings or doubts in these situations prior to or during the treatment process and be willing to discuss and deal with these issues. Rarely, but importantly, a provider may decide to refer the client to another professional, and this, too, should be discussed with the client with the options and the advantages and disadvantages explored before a decision is made.

When it appears to either or both the patient and the professional that the relevant goals have been attained and treatment is completed, the patient and the provider should discuss the option of termination or of continuing with additional treatment. Sometimes a patient will decide to tackle another issue, or the provider recognizes the need for addressing a related problem, and a discussion is necessary to set new goals, clarify expectations, determine criteria, and begin a new phase of treatment. Occasionally, new treatment issues arise and a patient would be better served by being referred to a different provider.

Once the patient feels that the goals have been achieved, the patient and the provider should discuss how termination will occur and the approximate number of visits it will take. When termination occurs, the therapeutic relationship is ended; usually this is with the understanding that, if the patient is in need of further assistance, they can call for an appointment in the future.

What happens if goals are not attained and treatment is not completed due to a decision on the part of the client or the provider? Sometimes clients will suddenly drop out of treatment or discuss with the provider their intention to quit before goals are achieved. The provider can outline the recent progress and accomplishments of the client and offer to continue when the client chooses to do so. The provider can also agree to the termination of treatment, in which case the therapist notifies the client and the PCP (or other referring source) in writing that treatment has been stopped as of a certain date and that the patient is no longer under the care of the treating professional. If the patient calls again to request continued treatment, it is up to the provider to decide if restarting the therapeutic relationship or referring the client elsewhere is in the client's best interest. Some medical insurance companies will also require notification of treatment terminations.

WHAT PATIENTS CAN DO TO HELP THEMSELVES

Stress Management

The concept of stress is often misunderstood, which is one of the reasons it is often difficult to implement stress management and follow through with appropriate treatment. Stress is not something negative that happens to us; rather, it is a psychological and physical response to an external or sometimes internal event, which means that anything that happens to us can produce a stress response. Frequently, stress management is an element of formal treatment, the goal being to help the patient to manage his or her life in healthier and more productive ways. Sometime this requires maintenance treatment once or twice a month for people with chronic conditions or who are in chronically stressful situations. Therapy for stress management maintenance can include:

1. Consolidating and reinforcing positive gains
2. Identifying new activities and opportunities
3. Monitoring symptoms and behavior for relapse, and tracking less productive patterns of behavior
4. Continuing stress management practices

Regardless of the psychological or medical problems, stress can always worsen or complicate the issues. Most people feel victimized by stress, as if there is nothing they can do about it. An important element of treatment is learning to recognize what you can and cannot control. The Serenity Prayer, which is attributed to theologian Reinhold Niebuhr and is used by Alcoholics Anonymous and other twelve-step programs, says it best:

God, grant me the serenity
To accept the things I cannot change,
The courage to change the things I can,
And the wisdom to know the difference.

The first rule of stress management is to assess the issues in your life that are causing problems and to focus your time and energy only on those things over which you have some control. Learning new ways to deal with the remaining difficult people and situations in your life, rather than trying to fix and change them all, is a less stressful and more sensible way to manage your life. The second rule of stress management is to develop a perspective toward perceived problems. The following popular phrase makes that point:

Don't sweat the small stuff, and almost all of it is small stuff.

I have heard this wise guidance offered many times, and it is certainly worth remembering.

Frequently, patients will feel completely overwhelmed—as if their lives are "out of control." They begin to feel like victims who are besieged by powers and forces they cannot combat. When people begin to feel helpless and hopeless they will often experience psychological symptoms such as anxiety and/or depression. Learning to manage the stress caused by these feelings and the circumstances that produce them is one of the basic fundamentals of stress management. The first step is to identify the source(s) of stress and determine if they can be either minimized or eliminated. However, often we cannot directly impact the source of the stress and, instead, must modify our response to it, thereby minimizing the negative effects upon us.

The second step when feeling overwhelmed is to review the list of things that need to be done and take care of one or two small items just to remove them from the list. Another tactic is to organize chores by time rather than task. Instead of saying, "I have to clean the house," one could say, "I am going to work on the house for two hours, then take a break and do something different." If the house gets cleaned in two hours, great, but if not it will still be there to finish later even if in the next day or so. Achieving small goals helps people to feel in control of their surroundings and to combat feelings of helplessness and hopelessness.

The stimulus that produces feelings of stress or anxiety is called a *stressor*. A stressor that produces a negative response causes *distress*, and a stressor that produces a positive response causes *eustress*—not a word most people will recognize because we usually think of stress as something bad. Any changes in our lives, including the positive ones, produce stress: graduating from school, starting a new job, having a baby, buying a house, family gatherings, etc. The net effect of stress upon a person includes the sum of both positive and negative types of stress and is cumulative and persistent. Stress doesn't simply disappear when a stressful situation is concluded; rather, the effects of stress can persist over time and may affect us physically, psychologically, and emotionally long after the stressful situation has passed. Unfortunately, this stress then will usually build up and get worse if something different is not done.

Managing anxiety and stress involves taking positive steps before something forces us to slow down and/or take medical leave due to health changes such as illness, depression, or anxiety. Strategies for effectively managing stress include:

- Exercise
  ○ regularly (at least three or four times per week)
  ○ vary the exercise activities; do things that you enjoy
  ○ start slowly and build up
  ○ check with your physician regarding exercise
  ○ schedule exercise times on your calendar before other appointments; don't make excuses—this needs to be a priority
- Relaxation
  ○ learn techniques for deep muscle relaxation, meditation, or yoga; CDs are available at bookstores that will teach relaxation and other related techniques; there are also apps on smart phones that can be very helpful as well
  ○ regularly (at least three times per week)
  ○ learn regulated breathing techniques
- Time management
  ○ use a formal or informal organizing strategy such as a calendar, journal, lists, a cell phone, a personal digital assistant, a computer that you can carry with you, etc.
  ○ prioritize; get the most important things taken care of, but remember, not everything has to be done today
  ○ do not overbook yourself—schedule time for rest
  ○ avoid time-wasters like TV and video games (a little is OK, but do not overdo it)
  ○ schedule short break periods throughout the day
  ○ organize chores by time rather than task

- Recreation—doing things just for fun
  - ○ do not try to convince yourself that chores and work are recreation unless you truly enjoy doing them
  - ○ activities enjoyed alone (hobbies, reading, listening to or playing music)
  - ○ activities enjoyed with a significant other (take a walk, go on a date, take a day or weekend trip, go on vacation)
  - ○ activities enjoyed with family or friends

Additional recommendations for dealing with anxiety and stress include:

- Stay socially involved and active—keep in touch with the people who are important to you, but do not overdo it
- Minimize or eliminate caffeine and other stimulants
- Minimize or eliminate depressant drugs like alcohol—they may initially have a calming effect but when they wear off, intensified anxiety or panic attacks will return
- Regulate sleep patterns
  - ○ get up at about the same time each day
  - ○ do not extend sleep on weekends by more than an hour
  - ○ get enough sleep
    - ▪ Do you wake up rested without an alarm clock?
    - ▪ Do you feel tired during the day?
    - ▪ Most Americans are sleep deprived, and it takes a toll on your health.
  - ○ do not nap during the day if it interferes with your ability to fall and stay asleep at night—rest periods are fine; if you do need a nap, do so at the same time each day and only for an hour
- Develop good nutrition
  - ○ talk to your physician or a nutritionist
  - ○ do not overeat carbohydrates: e.g., white pasta and bread, potatoes, other starches and sugars
  - ○ eat lots of vegetables, fruits, and proteins; they are your friends
  - ○ good nutrition is not punishment
    - ▪ eat fresh food rather than canned or processed when you can
    - ▪ minimize unhealthy snacks
    - ▪ eat meals and healthy snacks regularly; 5 or 6 small meals/snacks a day is healthier than 3 large meals
    - ▪ control portion sizes, use a smaller plate
    - ▪ drink lots of water

·   minimize saturated and animal fats, fried food, margarine, butter

I try to give my patients the strong message that their treatment and recovery are largely in their hands—I can help, but they have to do the daily work. The more they do, the sooner they will notice improvements and the better they will feel. I remember my grandmother giving me some very good advice: "Remember, moderation in all things." Do not overeat, overwork, overspend, overexercise, oversocialize, overdrink, etc., and recreational activities such as gambling and hobbies should be carefully monitored to avoid developing new problems. Successful management of anxiety and stress requires following a treatment plan and initiating changes. People who suffer from anxiety disorders have the ability, with assistance from a trained mental health provider, to establish new patterns in order to improve their lives, to feel better, and to be physically and mentally healthier.

Unfortunately, many patients feel like the person they are working with should "fix" them and make them better. As important as professional help is and can be, it is only a small part of the picture. If people want their lives to change they must be willing to try to do some things differently. Remember: "If nothing changes—nothing changes!" Whenever any of us want to try to change or improve our lives we have to first consider what we are going to do differently. To expect all of the stressful people around us to change so that we can feel better is probably not going to happen. If we want our lives to be different we have to look at ourselves as the person who needs to modify their behavior. It is sad to see people who are miserable, sitting around and continuing to make the same mistakes but still blaming everyone else for their problems and waiting for others to change. It is your life, and if you want it to be different then you have to take the responsibility to find ways to make the changes. Occasionally patients will say, "This is just the way I am." What this means is that they feel there is nothing they can do to make their lives better. This is where a trained professional can be helpful in showing the person ways to think and act differently so that they can change; it is not easy, but it is not impossible either.

9

⬦

Making Sense of It All

CHANGING CONCEPTIONS OF ANXIETY AND RELATED DISORDERS

The goal of this book is to provide a working definition for different types of anxiety disorders and useful explanations as to how they develop and are treated. In order to qualify for a formal or clinical diagnosis a significant number of specific and identifiable symptoms must create significant distress and/or interfere with daily normal functioning and must also exist over a particular period of time. Being diagnosed with one of these disorders requires much more than simply feeling anxious, obsessed, or worried, and it is not always easy to understand the differences between normal functioning and real psychological problems.

These disorders produce considerable misery in those who suffer from them, and they usually impact friends and family as well. In addition, anxiety disorders can result in a significant expense with the highest cost being the loss of work/school time and other indirect costs. Most of us will never experience feeling deathly afraid of something or being fearful of leaving home, but those with anxiety disorders deal with this daily.

Perhaps the most tragic aspect of anxiety disorders is that a large majority of patients do not have access to or receive the effective and appropriate treatments, especially in underdeveloped regions of the world. Unfortunately, anxiety disorders do not generate the public's interest through telethons and major fundraising programs for supporting research and treatment. It is important that we pay more attention to and focus on the disease burden of mental health problems like we do with other serious illnesses.

The progress of research in the treatment of anxiety disorders during the past few decades is quite impressive. The recent gains made in the development of effective and safe medications for anxiety disorders are changing the lives of many patients, and there will likely be additional breakthroughs in the near future. However, medications will still serve primarily to control the symptoms of anxiety disorders and will not likely have a curative role.

In addition, remarkable gains in the development and improvement of psychological approaches to treatment are making a significant impact. However, the key to providing appropriate treatment for anxiety disorders lies in the hands of the competent and trained professionals who can make a long-lasting difference in patients' lives. One of the challenges facing the mental health field is that there are not enough trained providers to meet the needs of people who require treatment, especially in the underserved areas such as rural and impoverished communities. It is embarrassing that our mental health treatment system has effective therapies available that could make a difference for many patients and their families, but there are too few professionals to meet their needs. I suggest that this is not just a mental health problem but rather a public health and social problem that affects us all.

New and potentially valuable medical treatments are emerging that will likely change the approach to treating these disorders. Unique medical and surgical treatments will, in the near future, provide options that will result in new ways of providing treatment, mostly in the area of relieving symptoms. Although they may not cure the specific disorder, these new treatments may return patients to a level of functioning that allows them a quality of life they may have never known before. Similarly, as we learn more about the potential role of genetics in establishing a predisposition for some of these disorders, a whole new world of treatment options will open. Hopefully, someday we will be able to genetically discover who might be high risk for certain conditions, such as anxiety disorders, and then modify the relevant genes to reduce the risk. Sound like science fiction? These potential genetic treatments will not reduce the risk to zero, but by lessening the risk even a few percentage points the potential benefits would be enormous. We can expect that breakthroughs in genetics, neurophysiology, neurochemistry, neuroimaging, as well as in psychology, psychopharmacology, and psychiatry will, in the future, offer new treatment approaches we have yet to imagine.

The lack of access to appropriate mental health treatments by many people, and not just those in the underserved areas and developing countries, is embarrassing. Since the early 1980s insurance companies have controlled access to medical and mental health care, and they have successfully reduced the number of mental health visits as well as the circumstances under which a person is able to be treated. It is not uncommon to discover that an insurance company will only cover the services of certain providers and specific diagnoses and will deny coverage for chronic or preexisting conditions that do not meet their definition of medical necessity. The mental health coverage in many of the insurance and managed care contracts is eliminated from coverage with these two little words: *medical necessity*. Hospitalization stays, beyond the first day, are decided primarily by insurance company employees, often turning ill and suffering patients back onto the streets or sending them home with loved ones who are scared and don't know how to handle the situation. Insurance will almost never cover educational testing and scholastic counseling, court-ordered testing and therapy in cases of divorce and custody disagreements, and rarely marital, family, or relationship counseling. Some insurance companies, including publicly funded ones like Medicare and Medicaid, will not provide a list of participating providers to callers, which leaves the responsibility of finding a mental health professional with the patient who must call office after office looking for someone who will accept them as a new patient. Medicaid used to offer a telephone number that patients could call to find a provider in their zip code area, but due to budget cuts, this service has not been available for over a decade. Of course, many people cannot afford insurance premiums at any level or do not qualify for public assistance, and they must continue without care for all types of illnesses. People in our communities, our neighbors, our children's classmates, our coworkers, and people in stores we frequent as well as on planes, trains, and buses are living without medical or mental health coverage. Clearly, the lack of adequate care for a large part of the population seriously affects us all in our daily lives. Politicians repeatedly claim they are trying to solve these problems, but in the past thirty years little progress has been evident.

One issue worth paying attention to is how thinking in the public, political, health, and mental health arenas, and even the media, evolve and change over time. In the recent past, professionals discussed "neuroses" and treatment options that were limited to a few (largely ineffective) pills and psychoanalytic psychotherapy. However, now we classify these illnesses as anxiety disorders, and treatment includes many different psychological therapies and medication choices. In reality, the types and availability of treatments depend more upon social factors than medical or psychological ones. How society regards health, mental health, diagnosis, treatment, and other related factors determines how public and private funds are used to provide care and who receives care. Interestingly, one of the primary reasons for a lack of mental health professionals is the substantial decrease in funding for training programs, scholarships, and education—clearly, social and political choices. In general, people are more aware of and knowledgeable about mental health issues than they have been in the past, but the levels of ignorance, misinformation, bias, and stigma are still substantial and serious issues.

COPING WITH ANXIETY DISORDERS

Dealing with anxiety disorders involves improving prevention, treatment, coping strategies, education and training, and social/political action. Preventing or at least reducing the frequency of anxiety disorders warrants our attention and, again, education is the critical issue. Although most physicians will recognize and treat patients with anxiety, many are not familiar with the variety and availability of new and effective treatments. Mental health professionals should be responsible for sharing this information and for informing physicians of how they can refer patients for the care they need. Preventing anxiety disorders, however, it is not so simple. Since the basis for many anxiety disorders is set during childhood, they usually involve early learning and even genetic predispositions, factors that cannot be changed easily, if at all. Certainly, we cannot modify a person's genetic endowment, although we may see it possible in the not too distant future. Similarly, we cannot change a person's history, but we can help them to learn from their past and to make changes today in ways that will help them to live healthier and happier lives. Treatment can also include learning to resist or recover from anxiety disorders that may have resulted from events in a patient's past.

Minimizing and/or preventing anxiety disorders often relies heavily on a person's lifestyle, their ability to deal with stress and conflict, and their exposure to traumatic or stressful circumstances. Stress management is a critical aspect of preventing or minimizing anxiety. Therefore, if a person

- gets enough sleep and rest,
- exercises regularly,

- has a healthy nutritional foundation,
- does not smoke,
- uses alcohol very sparingly, or not at all,
- avoids recreational drugs, like marijuana or cocaine,
- keeps stimulants to a minimum (including coffee and caffeinated soda),
- keeps a balanced lifestyle that includes recreation,
- is appropriately socially active,
- is productive at work/school but does not overdo or neglect other responsibilities,
- takes good care of themselves medically with regular physical exams,
- follows doctors' orders,
- seeks treatment when ill or injured,
- avoids problematic activities, like excessive gambling,
- effectively manages time,
- does not overextend themselves financially or in terms of activities, and
- schedules time for relaxation and enjoyment,

they will, then, have a reasonable chance of avoiding anxiety disorders.

The problem for most of us is maintaining balance in our lives, and it is easy to feel trapped and unable to do anything about it. However, as soon as we allow ourselves to feel victimized by those things over which we have no control, we will often give up hope of ever having a normal life, and we have lost the battle.

While trying to help a particular patient gain a sense of control in her life, I encouraged her to take short breaks at work and to make sure that she ate a nutritious lunch. This was a challenge for her since she had discussed the fear of not having enough time in the day to take short breaks or a lunch period. I assured her that the research literature strongly supports the claim that people who to take regular breaks at work are more efficient and more productive, but it was a hard sell. Finally, she grew sick and tired of feeling sick and tired, and she began to take breaks during her work day. Very quickly she discovered that she was feeling better and accomplishing more, and that her boss noticed and complimented her on taking better care of herself and on being a good role model for other employees—smart boss.

Frequently I hear the reverse argument from people who feel that it is impossible to make any reasonable changes in their lives and believe that they are completely trapped. They ask me to make them feel better but are unwilling to make any of the changes I suggest. Logically, of course, this makes no sense; how can someone expect to feel better when they are repeating the behaviors that are contributing to, if not causing, them to feel poorly? The goal of treatment is usually to help the patient to discover new ways of dealing with their concerns in order to realize better outcomes, but it also means that the patient must be receptive to a different way of thinking and acting that will help them.

Exercising daily is a relatively simple task that is enormously helpful in dealing with mental health conditions, and especially anxiety and/or mood disorders. Yet, I will frequently hear from patients, "I have no time to do it." Consider for a moment how a busy person will always find the time to add one more meeting or one more errand into their already crowded day/week. Each of us needs to identify blocks of time for taking care of ourselves *before* we fall victim to everyone else's scheduling needs. Our own good health must be a daily priority; others will respect such efforts, and it will be easier to consider making other necessary changes when you have better control of your time.

Dealing with and preventing anxiety and other related disorders boils down to two words: *balance* and *assertiveness*. Maintaining a well-balanced life includes meeting your responsibilities along with enjoying periods of relaxation, rest, recreation, exercise, and socialization. In order to achieve all of the above, efficiency is necessary. Efficiency means making the best use of our time but not allowing ourselves to become trapped in routines that feel like a hamster running on a wheel. It is okay, occasionally, to set aside a chore in order to take a walk with a spouse or throw a ball to a child or just sit and read for fifteen minutes. Efficiency also means avoiding time wasters, such as television and video games, a trap for many. Picking a few enjoyable shows to watch per week or playing a game for a short period of time is different from sitting for hours each day channel surfing, watching programs, and hanging on to a game remote just to kill time. Also, a couch potato will usually combine mindless viewing with eating junk food and drinking soda or alcohol, all of which have a significant negative impact on our health. It is absolutely frightening to read studies reporting that many children spend 4–7 hours *per day* watching TV or playing video games. This means that the majority of their lives, outside of school and sleeping, is spent in front of some form of electronic entertainment. It is essential, therefore, to make watching TV or playing video games a conscious choice rather than just a default activity. I constantly remind parents to place time limits on TV and video games both for themselves and for their children—and stick to it. No child's life has ever been ruined because they had to stop playing "Need for Speed" before they wanted to. Toddlers need quiet time to engage their imaginations and create stories with their toys and should not have a continuous droning of television audio in the background. They need to develop skills such as focusing and concentrating on the activity in which they are engaged, rather than be continuously interrupted by random loud noises.

Assertiveness, in our culture, is often confused with aggressiveness; being aggressive means to act in a manner that directly and negatively impacts or hurts another person or will establish dominance over them. Being assertive, on the other hand, means to behave in a manner that ensures your needs are met, but not necessarily at the expense of another person. I tell my patients that assertiveness simply means acting in ways that convey to others: "My needs are just as important as your needs; not more important, but not less important either." Frequently it is female patients who report feeling as if everyone else's needs must be met before they can do anything for themselves, which of course includes their children, spouse, partner, parents, etc. It is neither reasonable nor even possible to completely meet everyone else's needs and expectations, and it is important to understand that you will do a better job of taking care of others if you take care of yourself first. This is not being selfish; it is just a reality. Further, by assertively taking care of yourself you are modeling for others, including your children, as to how to avoid unhealthy patterns that define most people's lives and to maintain a balance that ensures we do the essential tasks and still have time for the fun.

BEING A POSITIVE VOICE FOR GOOD MENTAL HEALTH

The best way to be a positive voice for mental health is to be a good role model; that is doing the things that are necessary to keep yourself physically and mentally healthy. One challenge to making healthy and productive changes in your life is to alter the old dysfunctional patterns that are deeply ingrained habits. Making small but consistent steps and sticking to them is the best method; small changes begin to multiply until major changes occur and it becomes second nature. Often people try to do too much at once, and when they are not successful at everything they are trying to do, they just give up.

Speaking out publicly for mental health is also important, and there are numerous ways of accomplishing this in a positive and constructive manner. Writing to politicians and voting are good ways to exert influence, but it is often frustrating as well. When you talk to or write to politicians, their vague response will typically reflect the latest polls and include a reassuring message, basically telling you what you want to hear. More importantly, watch how they vote on issues concerning mental health legislation and actively work to elect someone else if they do not vote the way you would like. When you contact politicians it is important to let them know that you are a constituent and express your interests and preferences. Regardless of what they tell you, most politicians are primarily interested in being re-elected. Even if you are not of voting age, it is important to recognize that your voice counts as well. If you and others voice your concerns clearly on how you feel about certain issues, politicians will pay attention and perhaps you will see positive change.

In addition to contacting politicians, the message for the need of good mental health programs and practices must be carried to our schools, hospitals, and mental health facilities and programs. Teachers and school administrators wield considerable influence over our children for a substantial portion for most days in the year. Encouraging schools to support positive mental health through nutrition and public health education, good psycho-educational and psycho-social programs, and appropriate staffing is essential for good public health in our communities. Programs such as sports, music, drama, clubs, and outreach all help our children to become healthy, happy, and productive adults.

Mental health is closely aligned with physical health, which is largely dependent upon our health habits and what we eat as well as on our ability to exercise and enjoy sports and other activities. For the past two decades, childhood obesity has become a national epidemic, and insisting that all of our schools offer nutritious menu choices of low-fat, high fiber foods and eliminating soda and candy machines is a place to start. Having healthy food choices and good health practices within our own homes is also an important message to our children. Retaining physical education as part of the school curriculum not only gives students opportunities for physical activity, but it teaches them that daily exercise is important in order to stay active and healthy. Learning life-long sports, such as tennis, golf, cross-country skiing, basketball, volleyball, running/jogging, and bowling, is a way to convey to our children that it is possible and necessary to exercise as adults, even into the senior years. Similarly, learning to appreciate and participate in the fine arts, such as playing a musical instrument, singing, dancing, dramatic arts, sculpting, painting, and drawing, as well as learning to use technologies like computers in the arts and music, is also essential for a civilized and productive society. Businesses today are crying out for new ideas and employees who can creatively solve problems and generate innovative solutions. People who are broadly and liberally educated in a variety of areas in addition to the "four Rs" are the future employees, scientists, teachers, and professionals that our country and the world need.

Another example of helping to improve mental and social health in schools and society is to help deal with problems like physical and verbal abuse. For example, bullying in schools, workplaces, the home, and in public is finally being recognized for what it is: physical or verbal abusive behavior toward someone who cannot defend him- or herself. The more children and adults are held accountable for their behavior and potential victims feel that there is an avenue of recourse should they feel threatened or intimidated, then the fewer stress-related absences there will be in our schools and businesses. Organizations that are recognizing and dealing with these types of problems are showing the kinds of awareness and leadership that will help prevent some of the mental health problems of the future.

We can also be a positive influence in the workplace by making it a healthier and more productive part of our lives. Too often, businesses ignore the "people side" of the workplace, considering it a waste of time and money. Research convincingly demonstrates, however, that companies and organizations that take care of their employees are able to recruit and keep the best employees who in turn are more productive and satisfied with their jobs. Programs through the American Psychological Association and various state psychological associations support and annually recognize companies for having a psychologically healthy workplace and encourage policies that reduce stress and create a pleasant work environment. This is sometimes a hard sell to executives, and especially to those who say things like, "This is a tough business, and if an employee isn't tough enough to handle the job, then let them find another place to work." This sounds very harsh and almost makes sense, except that when an organization creates a stressful work environment, it will certainly lead to increased voluntary turnover, which means that employees quit and leave by their own choice. Executives and administrators should keep in mind that when voluntary turnover escalates, it is often the best employees who will leave first because they are good enough to find a job elsewhere and those who are underproducing or are not doing their job are the ones likely left behind.

Money spent to create a healthy work environment more than pays for itself in reduced turnover, higher productivity, and lower levels of absenteeism. Examples of meeting the human needs of employees might include things like having a fair wage; providing reasonable benefits including health insurance; onsite daycare for children of employees; maternity, paternity, and adoption leave; education benefits (paid time off to take classes or tuition reimbursement); training programs; health-related programs onsite (e.g., exercise, stop smoking groups, weight loss programs, and stress management); an employee assistance program; and some even have a wellness and exercise center on site. Although these programs may cost money, they usually turn out to be cost effective in the long run; this is not just good treatment of employees—this is good business.

MAKING A DIFFERENCE

Educating ourselves about issues of health and mental health, including anxiety and related disorders, is a place to start. Relying again on wisdom from the Twelve Step heritage, we have to "talk the talk," but even more importantly we have to "walk the walk." Educating others about the anxiety disorder that a family member or friend is dealing with is much more effective than simply complaining and whining about how insensitive and ignorant people can be. If we truly want to make a difference we must also reach out and help others who may not be able to help themselves. We must inform and educate people who may not know or understand psychological problems. This could include speaking with people who have similar conditions, getting involved with a self-help group, or even volunteering to give a speech to a group that would like to learn more about these disorders. Helping others is often a very good way to help ourselves, and we should always be on the alert for opportunities to do both.

The message that I want to leave with readers is: "We are only helpless if we allow ourselves to be." Bad and unfortunate events will happen to all of us at one time or another, but assuming the role of *victim* is a choice and one we should avoid. The role of victim traps us in situations where we feel passive and helpless, but taking responsibility for our own choices and health, as well as helping and supporting others to take control of their own lives, can result in our being a positive influence in our families and communities.

Appendix

Resources

There are many good places for people to find additional information about anxiety disorders, and we have identified some of them. In addition, there are websites as well as books and articles that might be of interest.

ORGANIZATIONS

American Psychiatric Association
1000 Wilson Blvd., Ste. 1825
Arlington, VA 22209-3901
703-907-7300/888-35-PSYCH
www.heathyminds.org

American Psychological Association
750 First St., NE
Washington, DC 20002-4242
800-374-2721/202-336-5500
www.apa.org

Anxiety Disorders Association of America
8730 Georgia Avenue, Ste. 600
Silver Spring, MD 20910
240-485-1001
www.adaa.org

National Alliance on Mental Illness
Colonial Place Three
2107 Wilson Blvd., Ste. 300
Arlington, VA 22201-3042
703-542-7600/800-950-6264
www.nami.org

National Institute of Mental Health
Science Writing, Press, and Dissemination Branch
6001 Executive Blvd.
Rm. 8184, MSC 9663
Bethesda, MD 20892-9663
866-615-6464/301-443-4513
www.nimh.nih.org

National Mental Health Association
2001 Beauregard St., 6th Floor
Alexandria, VA 22311
800-969-NMHA/703-684-7722
www.nmha.org

WEBSITES

Anxiety Centre. "Famous People Affected by an Anxiety Disorder."
     (2010), www.anxietycentre.com/anxiety-famous-people.shtml.
Healthy Place. "Anxiety in the Elderly." *HealthyPlace.com* (2007), http://
     www.healthyplace.com/anxiety-panic/main/anxiety-in-the-elderly
     .html.
Healthy Place. "Mental Health Problems among Minorities." *Healthy
     Place.com* (2002), http://www.healthyplace.com/anxiety-panic/main
     /mental-health-problems-among-minorities.
Healthy Place. "Women and Anxiety: Twice as Vulnerable as Men."
     (2007), http://www.healthyplace.com/anxiety-panic/main/women-and
     -anxiety.html.
Psychiatry.HealthSE.com. "Generalized Anxiety Disorder (GAD)." *Cur-
     rent Medical Diagnosis & Treatment in Psychiatry* (2005), http://psychia
     try.healthse.com/psy/more/generalised_anxiety_disorder_gad/.
Psychiatry.HealthSE.com. "Panic Disorder and Agoraphobia." *Current
     Medical Diagnosis & Treatment in Psychiatry* (2005), http://psychiatry
     .healthse.com/psy/more/panic_disorder_and_agoraphobia/.

Psychiatry.HealthSE.com. "Post-Traumatic Stress Disorder (PTSD)." *Current Medical Diagnosis & Treatment in Psychiatry* (2005), http://psychiatry.healthse.com/psy/more/post_traumatic_stress_disorder_ptsd/.

University of Maryland Medical Center. "Anxiety Disorders." *Medical References; Patient Education* (2008), http://www.umn.edu/patiented/articles/what_anxiety_disorders_000028-1.htm.

BOOKS AND ARTICLES

American Psychiatric Association. *Diagnostic and Statistical Manual, Fourth Edition, Text Revision.* Washington, DC: American Psychiatric Association, 2000.

Antony, M. M., and R. P. Swinson. *Phobic Disorders and Panic in Adults: A Guide to Assessment and Treatment.* Washington, DC: American Psychological Association, 2000.

Antony, M. M., and M. B. Stein, eds. *Handbook of Anxiety and Related Disorders.* New York: Oxford University Press, 2009.

Bandura, A. *Principles of Behavior Modification.* New York: Holt, Rinehart, & Winston, 1969.

Barlow, D. H. *Anxiety and Its Disorders: The Nature and Treatment of Anxiety and Panic,* 2nd ed. New York: Guilford Press, 2002.

Barlow, D. H., ed. *Clinical Handbook of Psychological Disorders.* New York: Guilford Press, 1993.

Beck, A. T., and G. Emery. *Anxiety Disorders and Phobias: A Cognitive Perspective.* New York: Basic Books, 1985.

First, M. B., and A. Tasman. *DSM-IV-TR Mental Disorders: Diagnosis, Etiology, and Treatment.* Hoboken, NJ: John Wiley & Sons, 2004.

Gabbard, G. O., ed. *Treatment of Psychiatric Disorders,* 3rd ed. Washington, DC: American Psychiatric Publishing, 2001.

Mowrer, O. H. "Stimulus Response Theory of Anxiety." *Psychological Review* 46 (1939): 553–65.

National Institute of Mental Health. "Anxiety Disorders." Washington, DC: National Institute of Mental Health, 2009.

Rachman, S. *Fear and Courage,* 2nd ed. New York: Freeman, 1990.

Swartz, K. I. "Depression and Anxiety." In *The Johns Hopkins White Papers.* Baltimore, MD: Johns Hopkins Medical School, 2007.

Swartz, K. I. "Depression and Anxiety." In *The Johns Hopkins White Papers.* Baltimore, MD: Johns Hopkins Medical School, 2008.

References

CHAPTER 1

Anxiety Centre, "Famous People Affected by an Anxiety Disorder." (2010), www.anxietycentre.com/anxiety-famous-people.shtml.

L. A. Clark and D. Watson, "Tripartite Model of Anxiety and Depression: Psychometric Evidence and Taxonomic Implications," *Journal of Abnormal Psychology* 100, no. 3 (1991): 316–36.

S. Freud, *New Introductory Lectures in Psychoanalysis*, edited by James Strachey, *The Complete Works of Sigmund Freud*. New York: W.W. Norton, 1965.

K. I. Swartz, "Depression and Anxiety," in *The Johns Hopkins White Papers*. Baltimore, MD: Johns Hopkins Medical School, 2007.

J. M. Twenge, "The Age of Anxiety? Birth Cohort Change in Anxiety and Neuroticism, 1952–1993," *Journal of Personality and Social Psychology* 79, no. 6 (2000): 1007–21.

University of Maryland Medical Center, "Anxiety Disorders," *Medical References; Patient Education* (2008), http://www.umn.edu/patiented/articles/what_anxiety_disorders_000028–1.htm.

CHAPTER 2

C. A. Alfano, "Sleep-Related Problems among Children and Adolescents with Anxiety Disorders," *Journal of the American Academy of Child and Adolescent Psychiatry* 46, (2007): 224–32.

American Psychiatric Association, *Diagnostic and Statistical Manual, Fourth Edition, Text Revision*. Washington, DC: American Psychiatric Association, 2000.

G. A. Brenes, "Age Differences in the Presentation of Anxiety," *Aging and Mental Health* 10, no. 3 (2006): 298–302.

G. A. Brenes, M. Knudson, W. V. McCall, J. D. Williamson, M. E. Miller, and M. A. Stanley, "Age and Racial Differences in the Presentation and Treatment of Generalized Anxiety Disorder in Primary Care," *Journal of Anxiety Disorders* 22, no. 7 (2008): 1128–36.

D. R. Brown, W. W. Eaton, and L. Sussman, "Racial Differences in Prevalence of Phobic Disorders," *Journal of Nervous and Mental Disease* 178, no. 7 (1990): 434–41.

H. Chen, P. Cohen, J. Johnson, and S. Kasen, "Psychiatric Disorders During Adolescence and Relationships with Peers from Age 17 to Age 27," *Social Psychiatry and Psychiatric Epidemiology* 44, no. 3 (2009): 223–30.

B. J. Cox, R. P. Swinson, I. D. Shulman, K. Kuch, and J. T. Reichman, "Gender Effects and Alcohol Use in Panic Disorder with Agoraphobia," *Behavioral Research and Therapy* 31, (1993): 413–16.

E. DeBeurs, A. T. F. Beekman, A. J. L. M. Van Baldom, D. J. H. Deeg, R. van Dyck, and W. van Tilburg, "Consequences of Anxiety in Older Persons: It's Effect on Disability, Well-Being and Use of Health Services," *Psychological Medicine* 29 (1999): 583–93.

C. C. Diala and C. Muntaner, "Mood and Anxiety Disorders among Rural, Urban, and Metropolitan Residents in the United States," *Community Mental Health Journal* 39, no. 3 (2003): 239–52.

R. L. Dupont, D. P. Rice, L. S. Miller, S. S. Sharaki, C. R. Rowland, and H. J. Harwood, "Economic Costs of Anxiety Disorders," *Anxiety* 2, no. 4 (1996): 167–72.

G. J. Emslie, "Pediatric Anxiety—Underrecognized and Undertreated," *New England Journal of Medicine* 359, no. 26 (2008): 2835–36.

P. E. Greenberg, T. Sisitsky, R. C. Kessler, S. T. Finkelstein, E. R. Berndt, J. R. T. Davidson, J. C. Ballenger, and A. J. Fyer, "The Economic Burden of Anxiety Disorders in the 1990s," *Journal of Clinical Psychiatry* 60 (1999): 427–35.

G. Ginsburg and K. L. Drake, "Anxiety Sensitivity and Panic Attack Symptomatology among Low-Income African-American Adolescents," *Journal of Anxiety Disorders* 16, no. 1 (2002): 83–96.

G. Ginsburg, M. Riddle, and M. Davies, "Somatic Symptoms in Children and Adolescents with Anxiety Disorders," *Journal of the American Academy of Child and Adolescent Psychiatry* 45, no. 10 (2006): 1179–87.

W.-C. Hwang and S. Goto, "The Impact of Perceived Racial Discrimination on the Mental Health of Asian American and Latino College Students," *Cultural Diversity and Ethnic Minority Psychology* 14, no. 4 (2008): 326–35.

G. Y. Iwamasa and K. M. Hilliard, "Depression and Anxiety among Asian American Elders: A Review of the Literature," *Clinical Psychology Review* 19, no. 3 (1999): 343–57.

C. G. Last, S. Perrin, M. Hersen, and A. E. Kazdin, "A Prospective Study of Childhood Anxiety Disorders," *Journal of the American Academy of Child and Adolescent Psychiatry* 35 (1996): 1502–10.

A. S. Lau, J. Fung, S. Wang, and S. Kang, "Explaining Elevated Social Anxiety among Asian Americans: Emotional Attunement and a Cultural Double Bind," *Cultural Diversity and Ethnic Minority Psychology* 15, no. 1 (2009): 77–85.

S. Okazaki, "Sources of Ethnic Differences between Asian American and White American College Students on Measures of Depression and Social Anxiety," *Journal of Abnormal Psychology* 106, no. 1 (1997): 52–60.

J. E. Pachankis and M.R. Goldfried, "Social Anxiety in Young Gay Men," *Journal of Anxiety Disorders* 20, no. 8 (2006): 996–1015.

R. E. Roberts, C. R. Roberts, and W. Chan, "One-Year Incidence of Psychiatric Disorders and Associated Risk Factors among Adolescents in the Community," *Journal of Child Psychology and Psychiatry* 50, no. 4 (2009): 405–15.

D. H. Rosmarin, E. J. Krumrei, and G. Anderson, "Religion as a Predictor of Psychological Distress in Two Religious Communities," *Cognitive Behavior Therapy* 38, no. 1 (2009): 54–64.

D. W. Sue, "Culture-Specific Strategies in Counseling: A Conceptual Framework," *Professional Psychology: Research and Practice* 21 (1990): 424–33.

CHAPTER 3

W. S. Agras, D. Sylvester, and D. Oliveau, "The Epidemiology of Common Fears and Phobias," *Comprehensive Psychiatry* 10 (1969): 151–56.

A. Bandura, *Principles of Behavior Modification.* New York: Holt, Rinehart, & Winston, 1969.

D. H. Barlow, *Anxiety and Its Disorders: The Nature and Treatment of Anxiety and Panic.* 2nd ed. New York: Guilford Press, 2002.

A. T. Beck and G. Emery, *Anxiety Disorders and Phobias: A Cognitive Perspective.* New York: Basic Books, 1985.

D. C. Beidel and S. M. Turner, *Childhood Anxiety Disorders: A Guide to Research and Treatment*. New York: Routledge, 2005.

M. E. Bouton, S. Mineka, and D. H. Barlow, "A Modern Learning Theory Perspective on the Etiology of Panic Disorder," *Psychological Review* 108 (2001): 4–32.

M. A. Bruch and R. G. Heimberg, "Differences in Perceptions of Parental and Personal Characteristics between Generalized and Nongeneralized Social Phobics," *Journal of Anxiety Disorders* 8 (1994): 155–68.

B. F. Chorpita and D. H. Barlow, "The Development of Anxiety: The Role of Control in the Early Environment," *Psychological Bulletin* 124, no. 1 (1998): 3–21.

M. G. Craske and H. B. David, "Panic Disorder and Agoraphobia," in *Clinical Handbook of Psychological Disorders*, edited by David H. Barlow, 1–47. New York: Guilford Press, 1993.

R. R. Crowe, D. L. Pauls, D. J. Slymen, and R. Noyes, "A Family Study of Anxiety Neurosis," *Archives of General Psychiatry* 37 (1980): 77–79.

J. A. Gray, "Issues in the Neuropsychology of Anxiety," in *Anxiety and the Anxiety Disorders*, edited by A. H. Tuma and J. D. Maser. Hillsdale, NJ: Erlbaum, 1985.

J. A. Gray and N. McNaughton, "The Neuropsychology of Anxiety: Reprise," in *Perspectives on Anxiety, Panic and Fear*, edited by D. A. Hope, 61–134. Lincoln: Nebraska University Press, 1996.

J. Kagan, J. S. Reznick, and N. Snidman, "Biological Bases of Childhood Shyness," *Science* 240 (1988): 167–71.

E. H. W. Koster, E. Fox, and C. MacLeod, "Introduction to the Special Section on Cognitive Bias Modification in Emotional Disorders," *Journal of Abnormal Psychology* 118, no. 1 (2009): 1–4.

R. J. McNally, *Panic Disorder: A Critical Analysis*. New York: Guilford Press, 1994.

R. F. McNally and H. Reese, "Information-Processing Approaches to Understanding Anxiety Disorders," in *Handbook of Anxiety and Related Disorders*, edited by Martin M. Antony and Murray B. Stein, 136–52. New York: Oxford University Press, 2009.

B. L. Milrod, F. N. Busch, A. M. Cooper, and T. Shapiro, "Manual of Panic-Focused Psychodynamic Psychotherapy." Washington, DC: American Psychiatric Association, 1997.

S. Rachman, "The Conditioning Theory of Fear-Acquisition: A Critical Examination," *Behavior Research and Therapy* 15 (1977): 583–89.

S. Rachman, *Fear and Courage*. 2nd ed. New York: Freeman, 1990.

S. Reiss and R.J. McNally, "The Expectancy Model of Fear," in *Theoretical Issues in Behavior Therapy*, edited by S. Reiss and R. R. Bootzin, 107–21. New York: Academic Press, 1985.

N. B. Schmidt, J. A. Richey, J. D. Buckner, and K.R. Timpano, "Attention Training for Generalized Social Anxiety Disorder," *Journal of Abnormal Psychology* 118, no. 1 (2009): 5–14.

S. Torgersen, "Genetic Factors in Anxiety Disorders," *Archives of General Psychiatry* 40, no. 10 (1983): 85–89.

S. M. Turner, D. C. Beidel, J. W. Borden, M. A. Stanley, and R. G. Jacob, "Social Phobia: Axis I and II Correlates," *Journal of Abnormal Psychology* 100 (1991): 102–6.

CHAPTER 4

American Psychiatric Association, *Diagnostic and Statistical Manual, Fourth Edition, Text Revision*. Washington, DC: American Psychiatric Association, 2000.

N. Amir, C. Beard, M. Burns, and J. Bomyea, "Attention Modification Program in Individuals with Generalized Anxiety Disorder," *Journal of Abnormal Psychology* 118, no. 1 (2009): 28–33.

J. H. Boyd, "Use of Mental Health Services for the Treatment of Panic Disorder," *American Journal of Psychiatry* 143 (1986): 1569–74.

F. N. Busch, B. L. Milrod, and L. S. Sandberg, "A Study Demonstrating Efficacy of a Psychoanalytic Psychotherapy for Panic Disorder: Implications for Psychoanalytic Research, Theory, and Practice," *Journal of the American Psychoanalytic Association* 57, no. 1 (2009): 131–48.

C. S. Carter and R.J. Maddock, "Chest Pain in Generalized Anxiety Disorder," *International Journal of Psychiatry in Medicine* 22, no. 3 (1992): 291–98.

D. M. Clark, "A Cognitive Approach to Panic," *Behavioral Research and Therapy* 24, (1986): 461–70.

W. W. Eaton, R. C. Kessler, H. U. Wittchen, W. J. Magee, "Panic and Panic Disorder in the United States," *American Journal of Psychiatry* 151 (1994): 413–20.

P. L. Fisher and A. Wells, "Psychological Models of Worry and Generalized Anxiety Disorder," in *Oxford Handbook of Anxiety and Related Disorders*, edited by Martin M. Antony, 225–37. New York: Oxford University Press, 2009.

P. E. Greenberg, T. Sisitsky, R. C. Kessler, S. N. Finkelstein, E. R. Berndt, J. R. T. Davidson, J. C. Ballenger, and A. J. Fyer, "The Economic

Burden of Anxiety Disorders in the 1990s," *Journal of Clinical Psychiatry* 60, no. 7 (1999): 427–35.

H. Hazlett-Stevens, L. D. Pruitt, and A. Collins, "Phenomenology of Generalized Anxiety Disorder," in *Oxford Handbook of Anxiety and Related Disorders*, edited by Martin M. Antony and Murray B. Stein, 47–55. New York: Oxford University Press, 2009.

D. A. Katerndahl and J. P. Realini, "Where Do Panic Attack Sufferers Seek Care?" *Journal of Family Practice* 40 (1995): 237–43.

M. G. Kushner, "Relationship between Alcohol Problems and Anxiety Disorders," *American Journal of Psychiatry* 153, no. 1 (1996): 139.

J. S. Markowitz, M.M. Weissman, R. Oullette, J. D. Lish, and G. Klerman, "Quality of Life in Panic Disorder," *Archives of General Psychiatry* 46 (1989): 984–82.

L. McCabe, J. Cairney, S. Veldhuizen, N. Herrmann, and D. L. Streiner, "Prevalence and Correlates of Agoraphobia in Older Adults," *American Journal of Geriatric Psychiatry* 14, no. 6 (2006): 515.

National Institute of Mental Health, "Anxiety Disorders." Washington, DC: National Institute of Mental Health, 2009.

T. P. S. Oei, K. Wanstall, and L. Evans, "Sex Differences in Panic Disorder and Agoraphobia,"

T. Ohtani, H. Kaiya, T. Utsumi, K. Inoue, N. Kato, and T. Sasaki. "Sensitivity to Seasonal Changes in Panic Disorder Patients," *Psychiatry and Clinical Neurosciences* 60, (2006): 379–83.

Psychiatry.HealthSE.com. "Generalized Anxiety Disorder (GAD)." *Current Medical Diagnosis & Treatment in Psychiatry* (2005), http://psychiatry.healthse.com/psy/more/generalised_anxiety_disorder_gad/.

R. M. Rapee, "Generalized Anxiety Disorder: A Review of Clinical Features and Theoretical Concepts," *Clinical Psychology Review* 11 (1991): 419–40.

S. Reiss and R.J. McNally, "The Expectancy Model of Fear," in *Theoretical Issues in Behavior Therapy*, edited by S. Reiss and R. R. Bootzin, 107–21. New York: Academic Press, 1985.

M. Robichaud and M. J. Dugas, "Psychological Treatment of Generalized Anxiety Disorder," in *Oxford Handbook of Anxiety and Related Disorders*, edited by Martin M. Antony and Murray B. Stein, 364–74. New York: Oxford University Press, 2009.

F. Rouillon, "Epidemiology of Panic Disorder," *Human Psychopharmacology* 12 (1997): S7–S12.

K. I. Swartz, "Depression and Anxiety," in *The Johns Hopkins White Papers*. Baltimore, MD: Johns Hopkins Medical School, 2007.

E. J. Teng, A. D. Chaison, S D. Bailey, J. D. Hamilton, and N. J. Dunn, "When Anxiety Symptoms Masquerade as Medical Symptoms: What

Medical Specialists Know About Panic Disorder and Available Psychological Treatments," *Journal of Clinical Psychology in Medical Settings* 15, no. 4 (2008): 314–21.

M. M. Weissman, "Panic Disorder: Impact on Quality of Life," *Journal of Clinical Psychiatry* 52 (1991): 6–9.

CHAPTER 5

M. M. Antony and R. P. Swinson, *Phobic Disorders and Panic in Adults: A Guide to Assessment and Treatment*. Washington, DC: American Psychological Association, 2000.

L. Baer and W. E. Minichiello, "Behavior Therapy for Obsessive-Compulsive Disorder," in *Obsessive-Compulsive Disorders: Theory and Management*, edited by M. A. Jenike, L. Baer, and W.E. Minichiello. St. Louis, MO: Year Book Medical Publishers, 1990.

I. J. Cohen and I. Galykner, "Towards an Integration of Psychological and Biological Models of Obsessive-Compulsive Disorder: Phylogenetics Considerations," *CNS Spectrums* 2, no. 10 (1997): 26–44.

G. C. Curtis, W. J. McGee, W. W. Eaton, H. U. Wittchen, and R. C. Kessler, "Specific Fears and Phobias: Epidemiology and Classification," *British Journal of Psychiatry* 173, (1998): 212–17.

G. C. L. Davey and S. Marzillier, "Disgust and Animal Phobias," in *Disgust and Its Disorders: Theory, Assessment, and Treatment Implications*, edited by B. O. Olatunje and D. McKay, 169–90. Washington, DC: American Psychological Association, 2009.

W. W. Eaton, A. Dryman, and M. M. Weissman, "Panic and Phobia: The Diagnosis of Panic Disorder," in *Psychiatric Disorders in America: The Epidemiologic Catchment Area Study*, edited by L.N. Robins and D. A. Reiger, 155–79. New York: Free Press, 1991.

N. A. Heiser, S. M. Turner, D. C. Beidel, and R. Roberson-Nay, "Differentiating Social Phobia from Shyness," *Journal of Anxiety Disorders* 23, no. 4 (2009): 469–76.

H. I. Leonard, M. C. Lenane, S. E. Swedo, D. C. Rettew, E. S. Gershon, and J. L. Rapoport, "Tics and Tourette's Disorder: A 2- to 7-Year Follow-up of 54 Obsessive-Compulsive Children," *American Journal of Psychiatry* 149, 9 (1992): 1233–51.

G. Nestadt, J. Samuels, M. Riddle, O. J. Bienvenu III, K-Y. Liang, M. LaBuda, J. Walkup, M. Grados, and R. Hoen-Saric, "A Family Study of Obsessive-Compulsive Disorder," *Archives of General Psychiatry* 57 (2000): 358–63.

D. L. Pauls, J. P. Alsobrook, W. Goodman, S. Rasmussen, and J.F. Leckman, "A Family Study of Obsessive-Compulsive Disorder," *American Journal of Psychiatry* 152 (1995): 76–84.

D. L. Pauls, K. E. Towbin, J. F. Leckman, G. E. P. Zahner, and D. J. Cohen, "Gilles De La Tourette's Syndrome and Obsessive-Compulsive Disorder: Evidence Supporting a Genetic Relationship," *Archives of General Psychiatry* 43 (1986): 1180–82.

Psychiatry.HealthSE.com. "Specific Phobias." *Current Medical Diagnosis & Treatment in Psychiatry* (2005), http://psychiatry.healthse.com/psy/more/specific_phobias/.

S. A. Rasmussen and J. L. Eisen, "Phenomenology of Obsessive-Compulsive Disorder," in *Psychology of Obsessive-Compulsive Disorder*, edited by J. Insel and S. Rasmussen, 743–58. New York: Springer-Verlag, 1991.

K. Swartz, "Depression and Anxiety," in *The Johns Hopkins White Papers*. Baltimore, MD: Johns Hopkins Medical School, 2007.

S. E. Swedo, J. L. Rapoport, J. Leonard, M. Lenane, and D. Cheslow, "Obsessive-Compulsive Disorder in Children and Adolescents: Clinical Phenomenology of 70 Consecutive Cases," *Archives of General Psychiatry* 46 (1989): 335–41.

C. L. Turk, R. G. Heimberg, S. M. Orsillo, C. S. Holt, A. Gitow, L. L. Street, F. R. Schneier, and M. R. Liebowitz, "An Investigation of Gender Differences in Social Phobia," *Journal of Anxiety Disorders* 12 (1998): 209–23.

S. M. Turner, D. C. Beidel, and R. M. Townsley, "Social Phobia: A Comparison of Specific and Generalized Subtype and Avoidant Personality Disorder," *Journal of Abnormal Psychology* 101, no. 2 (1992): 326–31.

CHAPTER 6

American Psychiatric Association, *Diagnostic and Statistical Manual, Fourth Edition, Text Revision*. Washington, DC: American Psychiatric Association, 2000.

N. Breslau, "The Epidemiology of Posttraumatic Stress Disorder: What Is the Extent of the Problem?" *Journal of Clinical Psychiatry* 62 (2001): 16–22.

J. R. Davidson, L. A. Tupler, W. H. Wilson, and K. M. Connor, "A Family Study of Chronic Posttraumatic Stress Disorder Following Rape Trauma," *Journal of Psychiatric Research* 32 (1998): 301–9.

A. G. Harvey and R. A. Bryant, "Dissociative Symptoms in Acute Stress Disorder," *Journal of Traumatic Stress* 12, no. 573–680 (1999).

R. B. Hidalgo and J. R. T. Davidson, "Selective Serotonin-Reuptake Inhibitors in Post-Traumatic Stress Disorder," *Journal of Psychopharmacology* 14, no. 1 (2000): 70–76.

R .C. Kessler, A. Sonnega, E. Bromet, M. Hughes, and C. B. Nelson, "Posttraumatic Stress Disorder in the National Comorbidity Survey," *Archives of General Psychiatry* 52 (1995): 1048–60.

T. Lundin, "The Treatment of Acute Trauma: Posttraumatic Stress Disorder Prevention," *Psychiatric Clinics of North America* 17 (1994): 385–91.

M. C. Miller, "Preventing PTSD," edited by Michael Craig Miller. Boston: Harvard Mental Health Letter, 2009.

C. M. Monson, "Conjoint Treatment for PTSD," in *Second Annual Posttraumatic Stress Disorder Symposium*, 2–3. Cleveland, OH: Audio-Digest Psychiatry, 2007.

F. H. Norris, "Epidemiology of Trauma: Frequency and Impact of Different Potentially Traumatic Events on Different Demographic Events," *Journal of Consulting and Clinical Psychology* 60 (1992): 409–18.

R. V. Nydegger, L. A. Nydegger, and F. Basile, "Posttraumatic Stress Disorder and Coping in Career Professional Firefighters," paper presented at the International Business and Economic Research Conference, Las Vegas, October 2010.

D. S. Riggs and E. B. Foa, "Psychological Treatment of Posttraumatic Stress Disorder and Acute Stress Disorder," in *Oxford Handbook of Anxiety and Related Disorders*, edited by Martin M. Antony and Murray B. Stein. New York: Oxford University Press, 2009.

P. P. Schnurr and M. K. Jankowski, "Physical Health and Posttraumatic Stress Disorder: Review and Synthesis," *Seminars in Clinical Neuropsychiatry* 4 (1999): 295–304.

A. Shalev, A. Bleich, and R. J. Ursano, "Posttraumatic Stress Disorder: Somatic Comorbidity and Effort Tolerance," *Psychosomatics* 31 (1990): 197–303.

S. D. Solomon, E. T. Gerrity, and A. M. Muff, "Efficacy of Treatments for Posttraumatic Stress Disorder: An Empirical Review," *Journal of the American Medical Association* 268 (1992): 633–38.

G. Warda and R. A. Bryant, "Thought Control Strategies in Acute Stress Disorder," *Behavior Research and Therapy* 36 (1998): 1171–75.

D. S. Weiss, "Posttraumatic Stress Disorder: Part 1," in *PTSD: In an Age of Violence, Terror, and Disaster*, 1–3. San Francisco: Audio-Digest Psychiatry, 2008.

CHAPTER 7

J. J. Arch and M. G. Craske, "Acceptance and Commitment Therapy and Cognitive Behavioral Therapy for Anxiety Disorders: Different Treatments, Similar Mechanisms?" *Clinical Psychology: Science and Practice* 15, no. 4 (2008): 263–79.

P. Barrett and L. Farrell, "Prevention of Child and Youth Anxiety and Anxiety Disorders," in *Oxford Handbook of Anxiety and Related*

Disorders, edited by M. M. Antony and M. B. Stein, 497–511. New York: Oxford University Press, 2009.

F. N. Busch and B. Milrod, "Psychodynamic Treatment of Panic Disorder," in *Handbook of Evidence-Based Psychodynamic Psychotherapy: Bridging the Gap between Science and Practice*, edited by R. A. Levy and J. S. Ablon, 29–44. Totowa, NJ: Humana Press, 2009.

A. Carr, "The Effectiveness of Family Therapy and Systemic Interventions for Adult-Focused Problems," *Journal of Family Therapy* 31, no. 1 (2009): 46–74.

D. A. Chavira, M. B. Stein, and P. Roy-Hyrne, "Managing Anxiety in Primary Care," in *Oxford Handbook of Anxiety and Related Disorders*, edited by Martin M. Antony and Murray B. Stein, 512–22. New York: Oxford University Press, 2009.

J. L. Eagle, "Engaging the 'Wise Mind' of a Teen: Incorporating Mindfulness Practice into a Group Therapy Protocol for Anxious Adolescents," Massachusetts School of Professional Psychology, 2009.

M. G. Kushner, "Relationship between Alcohol Problems and Anxiety Disorders," *American Journal of Psychiatry* 153, no. 1 (1996): 139.

I. M. Marks, *Fears, Phobias, and Rituals*. New York: Oxford University Press, 1987.

R. E. McCabe and S. Gifford, "Psychological Treatment of Panic Disorder and Agoraphobia," in *Handbook of Anxiety and Related Disorders*, edited by M. M. Antony and M.B. Stein, 308–20. New York: Oxford University Press, 2009.

D. A. Moskovitch, M. M. Antony, and R. P. Swinson, "Exposure-Based Treatments for Anxiety Disorders: Theory and Process," in *Oxford Handbook of Anxiety and Related Disorders*, edited by M. M. Antony and M. B. Stein, 461–75. New York: Oxford University Press, 2009.

National Institute of Mental Health, "Anxiety Disorders," Washington, DC: National Institute of Mental Health, 2009.

P. J. Norton, "Integrated Psychological Treatment of Multiple Anxiety Disorders," in *Oxford Handbook of Anxiety and Related Disorders*, edited by Martin M. Antony and Murray B. Stein. New York: Oxford University Press, 2009.

T. H. Ollendick, L. G. Ost, L. Reuterskiold, N. Costa, R. Cederland, S. Sirbu, T.E. Davis III, and M. A. Jarrett, "One-Session Treatment of Specific Phobias in Youth: A Randomized Clinical Trial in the United States and Sweden," *Journal of Consulting and Clinical Psychology* 77, no. 3 (2009): 504–16.

M. W. Otto, E. Behar, J. A. J. Smits, and S. G. Hoffman, "Combining Pharmacological and Cognitive Behavioral Therapy in the Treatment of

Anxiety Disorders," in *Oxford Handbook of Anxiety and Related Disorders*, edited by Martin M. Antony and Murray B. Stein. New York: Oxford University Press, 2009.

L. Roemer, S. M. Erisman, and S. M. Orsillo, "Mindfulness and Acceptance-Based Treatments for Anxiety Disorders," in *Oxford Handbook of Anxiety and Related Disorders*, edited by M. M. Antony and M. B. Stein. New York: Oxford University Press, 2009.

B. O. Rothbaum, E. A. Meadows, P. Resick, and D. W. Foy, "Cognitive-Behavioral Therapy," in *Effective Treatments for PTSD: Practice Guidelines from the International Society for Traumatic Stress Studies*, edited by M. J. Friedman, 320–25. New York: Guilford Press, 2000.

J. Siev, "Specificity of Treatment Effects: Cognitive Therapy and Relaxation for Generalized Anxiety and Panic Disorders," *Journal of Consulting and Clinical Psychology* 76, no. 5 (2007): 513–22.

R. E. Steward, "Cognitive-Behavioral Therapy for Adult Anxiety Disorders in Clinical Practice: A Meta-Analysis of Effectiveness Studies," *Journal of Consulting and Clinical Psychology* 77 (2009): 595–606.

R. E. Stewart and D. L. Chambless, "Cognitive-Behavioral Therapy for Adult Anxiety Disorders in Clinical Practice: A Meta-Analysis of Effectiveness Studies," *Journal of Consulting and Clinical Psychology* 77 (2009): 595–606.

K. Swartz, "Depression and Anxiety," in *The Johns Hopkins White Papers*. Baltimore, MD: Johns Hopkins Medical School, 2007.

K. L. Swartz, "Depression and Anxiety," in *The Johns Hopkins White Papers*. Baltimore, MD: Johns Hopkins Medical School, 2008.

D. J. Van Ingen, S. R. Freiheit, and C. S. Vye, "From the Lab to the Clinic: Effectiveness of Cognitive-Behavioral Treatments for Anxiety Disorders," *Professional Psychology: Research and Practice* 40, no. 1 (2009): 69–74S.

J. J. Wood and B. D. McLeod, eds. *Child Anxiety Disorders: A Family-Based Treatment Manual for Practitioners*. New York: Norton, 2008.

CHAPTER 8

I. M. Aderka, "Factors Affecting Treatment Efficacy in Social Phobia: The Use of Video Feedback and Individual vs. Group Formats," *Journal of Anxiety Disorders* 23, no. 1 (2009): 12–17.

N. Amir, C. Beard, M. Burns, and J. Bomyea, "Attention Modification Program in Individuals with Generalized Anxiety Disorder," *Journal of Abnormal Psychology* 118, no. 1 (2009): 28–33.

S. Andres, L. Lazaro, M. Salamero, T. Boget, R. Penades, and J. Castro, "Changes in Cognitive Dysfunction in Children and Adolescents with

Obsessive-Compulsive Disorder after Treatment, *Journal of Psychiatric Research* 42, no. 6 (2008): 507–14.

J. C. Ballenger, J. R. T. Davidson, Y. Lecrubier, D. J. Nutt, T. D. Borkovec, K. Rickels, K. J. Stein, and H-U. Wittchen, "Consensus Statement on Generalized Anxiety Disorder from the International Consensus on Depression and Anxiety," *Journal of Clinical Psychiatry* 62 (Suppl. 11) (2001): 53–58.

O. Brawman-Mintzer and R. B. Lydiard, "Psychopharmacology of Anxiety Disorders," *Psychiatric Clinics of North America* 1 (1994): 51–79.

D. Direnfeld, M. T. Pato, and S. Gunn, "Behavior Therapy as Adjuvant Treatment in OCD," in *American Psychological Association Annual Meeting*. Chicago, 2000.

J. H. Greist, "Behavior Therapy for Obsessive-Compulsive Disorder," *Journal of Clinical Psychiatry* 55 (Suppl.) (1994): 36–43.

Harvard Mental Health Letter, "Combination Therapy for Panic Disorder," in *Harvard Mental Health Letter*, 4–5: Harvard Medical School, 2008.

J. D. Herbert, B. A. Gaudiano, A. A. Rheingold, E. Moitra, V H. Myers, K. L. Dalrymple, and L. L. Brandsma, "Cognitive Behavior Therapy for Generalized Social Anxiety Disorder in Adolescents: A Randomized Controlled Trial," *Journal of Anxiety Disorders* 23, no. 2 (2009): 167–77.

M. A. Jenike, "Pharmacotherapy of Obsessive-Compulsive Disorders," in *Psychopharmacology*. Boston, MA: Harvard Medical School, 1994.

P. Mansell and J. Read, "Post-Traumatic Stress Disorder, Drug Companies, and the Internet," *Journal of Trauma and Dissociation* 10, no. 1 (2009): 9–23.

R. E. McCabe and S. Gifford, "Psychological Treatment of Panic Disorder and Agoraphobia," in *Handbook of Anxiety and Related Disorders*, edited by M. M. Antony and M. B. Stein, 308–20. New York: Oxford University Press, 2009.

F. McManus, D. M. Clark, N. Grey, J. Wild, C. Hirsch, M. Fennell, A. Hackmann, L. Waddington, S. Liness, and J. Manley, "A Demonstration of the Efficacy of Two of the Components of Cognitive Therapy for Social Phobia," *Journal of Anxiety Disorders* 23, no. 4 (2009): 496–503.

T. H. Ollendick, L-G. Ost, L. Reuterskiold, N. Costa, R. Cederland, S. Sirbu, T. E. Davis III, and M. A. Jarrett, "One-Session Treatment of Specific Phobias in Youth: A Randomized Clinical Trial in the United States and Sweden," *Journal of Consulting and Clinical Psychology* 77, no. 3 (2009): 504–16.

G. O'Sullivan and I. Marks, "Follow-up Studies of Behavioral Treatment of Phobia and Obsessive-Compulsive Neurosis," *Psychiatric Annals* 21 (1991): 368–73.

L. Roemer, S. M. Orsillo, and K. Salters-Pednealt, "Efficacy of an Acceptance-Based Behavior Therapy for Generalized Anxiety Disorder: Evaluation in a Randomized Controlled Trial," *Journal of Consulting and Clinical Psychology* 76, no. 6 (2008): 1083–89.

K. Swartz, "Depression and Anxiety," in *The Johns Hopkins White Papers*. Baltimore, MD: Johns Hopkins Medical School, 2007.

M. L. Whittal, M. Robichaud, D. S. Thordarson, and P. D. McLean, "Group and Individual Treatment of Obsessive-Compulsive Disorder Using Cognitive Therapy and Exposure Plus Response Prevention: A 2-Year Follow-up of Two Randomized Trials," *Journal of Consulting and Clinical Psychology* 76, no. 6 (2008): 1003–14.

Index

About the Author

Rudy Nydegger, PhD, ABPP, is a board certified clinical psychologist, a professor emeritus of psychology at Union College, and a professor emeritus of management at the School of Management at Union Graduate College. He is also presently the chair of the Division of Psychology at Ellis Hospital in Schenectady, New York. He has practiced, taught, done research, and written about psychology for over forty years and is continuing to do so today. In addition, he is the immediate past-president and chair of the Board of the National Register of Health Service Psychologists. He is also past-president of the New York State Psychological Association and the Psychological Association of Northeastern New York. Further, he is a past board member of the New York State Board of Psychology. He has written books on depression, anxiety, and suicide and is coauthor of a book on workplace violence. He has contributed many chapters in books, sections in encyclopedias, and scholarly articles.

Date Due

MAY 2 7 2016		
NOV 0 1 2016		